Organizing to Count

JANET L. NORWOOD

ORGANIZING TO COUNT

Change in the Federal Statistical System

THE URBAN INSTITUTE PRESS
Washington, D.C.

BAS 2534 - 7/1

E URBAN INSTITUTE PRESS
0 M Street, N.W.
shington, D.C. 20037

itorial Advisory Board
lliam Gorham
iig G. Coelen
ele V. Harrell
rilyn Moon

Demetra S. Nightingale
George E. Peterson
Felicity Skidmore

Library of Congress Cataloging in Publication Data

Organizing to Count: Change in the Federal Statistical System / Janet L. Norwood.

1. United States—Statistical Services.
I. Title.

HA37.USSN67   1995   95-7967
353.0081'9—dc20   CIP

ISBN 0-87766-635-0 (paper, alk. paper)
ISBN 0-87766-634-2 (cloth, alk. paper)

Printed in the United States of America.

Distributed by: University Press of America

4720 Boston Way   3 Henrietta Street
Lanham, MD 20706   London   WC2E 8LU   ENGLAND

THE URBAN INSTITUTE is a nonprofit policy research and educational organization established in Washington, D.C., in 1968. Its staff investigates the social and economic problems confronting the nation and public and private means to alleviate them. The Institute disseminates significant findings of its research through the publications program of its Press. The goals of the Institute are to sharpen thinking about societal problems and efforts to solve them, improve government decisions and performance, and increase citizen awareness of important policy choices.

Through work that ranges from broad conceptual studies to administrative and technical assistance, Institute researchers contribute to the stock of knowledge available to guide decision making in the public interest.

Conclusions or opinions expressed in Institute publications are those of the authors and do not necessarily reflect the views of staff members, officers or trustees of the Institute, advisory groups, or any organizations that provide financial support to the Institute.

ACKNOWLEDGMENTS

My longstanding interest in the subject of this book and the ideas expressed in it have been developed and honed over many years in discussions with friends and colleagues. I am indebted first of all to the staff of the Bureau of Labor Statistics and especially to William Barron, Deborah Klein, Ronald Kutscher, Thomas Plewes, and Edwin Dean for their willingness to argue issues and for their insights into the broader aspects of the management of the federal statistical system. I have also benefited from discussion with my friends in other statistical agencies—in particular, Daniel Levine, Charles Waite, William Butz, and Harry Scarr at the Bureau of the Census, Carol Carson at the Bureau of Economic Analysis, and Emerson Elliot at the National Center for Educational Statistics—and the many others in the system who encouraged this work and assisted with information. I value as well discussions on this topic with friends in the statistical profession and at the American Statistical Association, including Stephen Fienberg, Miron Straf, Carolee Bush, Barbara Bailar, Fritz Scheuren, Judith Tanur, Mary Grace Kovars, Vincent Barabba, and John Rolph.

I am especially grateful to Katherine Wallman and to Hermann Habermann who read and commented in detail on an earlier draft, and to Felicity Skidmore, whose wisdom as an editor would be difficult to surpass. I also appreciate the support provided by the Urban Institute and to the Institute from the Bureau of the Census, Bureau of Justice Statistics, National Center for Educational Statistics, Bureau of Economic Analysis, National Agricultural Statistical Service, and the Economic Research Service.

CONTENTS

Tables

Figure

Ever since its founding a quarter century ago, the Institute has emphasized the crucial importance of improving not only the knowledge base underlying the way public policy is designed and evaluated, but also the administrative structure and process by which government carries out its responsibilities. *Organizing to Count: Change in the Federal Statistical System* brings both these aspects of the Institute's mandate together.

This book traces out the development of the U.S. federal statistical system, shows how it has grown by leaps and bounds over the years but with virtually no organizing framework, and underlines how, in the recent period of budget retrenchment, its resources have shrunk as its mandate and responsibilities have increased. It argues, furthermore, that the United States—whose statistical system once led the developed world—is in danger of falling behind other countries in its system's organizational efficiency and responsiveness to public and private needs for statistical information.

Many commissions and committees have evaluated the system through the years and made recommendations for its improvement. Their diagnoses of the problems have shared many similarities, by and large, as have their recommendations. But little has been done. Janet Norwood believes the time may have come when the nation is ready to pay attention to the needs of its federal statistical system and to summon the will to make necessary changes—not only in the way some statistics are collected, but more fundamentally in the organizational structure that defines responsibility for federal data collection as a whole.

In her words, "Before we can deal with . . . problems . . . we must understand the way things work, determine what needs repair, and finally decide how best to deal with the problem in a practical and realistic manner." There is more than one intelligent way to go about reforming the system, and the political process will make the final selection. This book is intended to help the American public and its policymakers understand the strengths and weaknesses of the current statistical system and how it is organized, so that they can build on that understanding to produce effective change.

William Gorham
President

Much of this book is the result of my experience as Commissioner of one of the largest statistical agencies in the federal government. During my quarter of a century at the Bureau of Labor Statistics, I became convinced that we need to improve the manner in which the statistical system functions. Over that period, government and private use of statistical information has increased considerably. Today, data produced by the federal statistical system are used in our tax laws and pension programs, decisions on defense expenditures, environmental protection, and education and training as well as in policy determination and evaluation of results. Now, after more than a decade of budget restraint and data retrenchment, it is clear that the statistical system must take steps to ensure that the national database moves forward to provide the country with the data it needs. In pursuing this objective, however, those interested in statistics tend to focus their efforts on the need for dollars to defray the cost of new surveys and redesign of existing surveys and to pay for the incorporation of more modern statistical methodology and more sophisticated technology. Of course, budgets are important. The nation's statistical budget could—and probably should—be increased. But it is time to recognize that we have problems in allocating the dollars already appropriated, and that we could do a much better job with what we have. It is time also to consider whether the system itself isn't part of the problem, and whether radical reorganization is needed and, if not, whether some simple yet important changes could make the system function more effectively and efficiently.

We must deal with a number of issues. First is the increasing fragmentation of the system. We have a system in the United States in which each new statistical agency that is created is placed in its own subject matter department where the Cabinet Officer in charge generally has neither the interest nor the knowledge to make trade-offs among the data programs in his own agency and those elsewhere in the government. We are unwilling to invest the power and resources required for coordination and oversight of the statistical system, and yet we have a tendency to multiply agencies to produce statistics. Moreover, this fragmentation is not limited to the Executive Branch of government. A myriad of different congressional committees have substantive and appropriations jurisdiction over the agencies that make up the federal statistical system.

Second, as the need for data has grown, a great deal of data collection is done outside those government agencies that count development and analysis of statistics as their primary mission. And review and control of the quality and validity of this work is limited and at times almost nonexistent. As a result, both public and private users of data find it increasingly difficult to get the data they need, and, when they are successful in their search, too often the data seem impossible to use. This is especially true when a user finds it necessary to integrate data collected by one statistical agency with those collected by another.

Finally, representation of the U.S. statistical system to other countries directly and through international organizations is also spread among a large number of federal agencies. The Statistical Policy Branch at the Office of Management and Budget represents the United States at the United Nations Statistical Commission. But unlike the arrangements in other countries, the Branch has virtually no staff to coordinate the international activities of each of the individual statistical agencies. Official statisticians in other countries, especially those with centralized systems, find communication with the very decentralized American system extremely difficult.

Before we can deal with such problems, however, we must understand the way things now work, then determine what needs repair, and finally decide how best to deal with the problems in a practical and realistic manner. I tackle all three tasks in this book. I start with a statement of the problems the federal statistical system now faces, its organizational structure and history, and the proposals of the many commissions and study groups that have recommended changes in the structure and authority of the system. I then compare the organization of the U.S. system with the highly centralized system in Canada and the decentralized system of the United Kingdom. I end by laying out proposed solutions and considering the chances for bringing about change in the current political environment.

In a democratic society, public policy choices can be made intelligently only when the people making the decisions can rely on accurate and objective statistical information to inform them of the choices they face and the results of the choices they make. The United States already lags behind other countries in the organizational efficiency and responsiveness of the system that produces such information. It is time to face the difficult issues involved and develop practical solutions to them.

Chapter One

INTRODUCTION

Information produced by the federal statistical system affects Americans in every aspect of their lives. The income we receive and the taxes we pay are adjusted by government price statistics. Every year, for example, the government adjusts social security and other pension payments for inflation and raises the levels of income to which progressively increased tax rates apply. Employment and productivity statistics help us to monitor the direction of our economy. Unemployment and income statistics help us to assess the condition of the labor market and the problems workers face. Statistical data help us to monitor our collective health, the purity of our air and water, and the economic well-being of our children. We use official statistics as tools to analyze financial markets, negotiate trade arrangements with other countries, and determine the size of federal grants to states and localities. Voting districts are based on local area data from the decennial Census. The Federal Reserve Board uses national accounts, price, and employment data in its decisions affecting the interest rates that help dictate the overall level of economic activity. Congress and the Administration use the Consumer and Producer Price Indexes to adjust entitlement programs, taxes, and expenditures on defense and other government procurement.

Yet despite the great power of statistical programs over the functioning of our public life, very few Americans know how official statistics are collected and compiled, and even less about the organization of the government agencies that produce them. When preliminary data series are revised, or when the numbers do not confirm our notions about the state of our world, we question the accuracy of official statistics. We complain that the official unemployment rate includes too few of those suffering economic hardship or too many of those who have not been out of work very long. We insist that the Consumer Price Index overstates the rate of inflation because it inadequately adjusts for changes in the quality of the products we buy, and some of us argue that the economy is growing at a faster—or slower—pace than the Gross Domestic Product figures show. The criticism often heats up at election time, when our statistical system is assailed as biased or incompetent, depending on whose ox is being gored by the current statistical trends.

Recently, as Americans have become increasingly concerned about the difficult problems in the economic and social structure of the country, criticism of the statistical system has focused more clearly on issues of data quality. *Business Week*, for example, has referred to "Washington's misleading maps of the economy," argued that " . . . the official figures may be badly out of whack" (June 3, 1991, p. 112), and complained that ". . . the real economy is vastly different from the one painted by the government's numbers" (November, 1994, p. 110). Economists focus on such issues as deficiencies in statistics about international capital and product flows, the undercount of the population census, inadequate representation of high technology products, outdated classification structures, and the lack of data coverage of the service-producing sector (Duncan 1991).

Virtually every commentary or expression of concern about the federal statistical system has included discussion of the need for more long-range planning of data products and better budgeting of data production. Concerns are also expressed about inefficiency in the use of resources, duplication of statistical output produced by different government agencies, as well as the slowness with which the system adjusts data to changes in the policy environment or to insights learned from academic research. And almost all have addressed the difficult task for users who need to put data produced in different parts of the system together into a single consistent framework (Bonnen 1984, Fienberg 1983, and Juster 1988). Although some may disagree about causes and solutions, there is, in fact, little disagreement about the diagnosis of the system's problems. As the Bonnen report put it:

> Until there is a substantial capacity to manage, coordinate and plan national data and analysis needs, we will lack "a place to stand" in facing the issues which now persist and grow in their threat to our ability to make intelligent policy decisions from good analysis founded on accurate, objective and relevant data bases. (President's Project 1981, p. 144)

Whether the discussion is about the incompatibility of data used in the national accounts and, therefore, the problems of integrating data produced by different agencies for different purposes (Report of NABE 1988) or the relevance of data to government policy needs, the problems inherent in the current statistical infrastructure have been recognized. Some focus attention on the system's inefficient determination of resource allocation[1] when decisions on what, how, and when to produce statistical series are generally made in each department with priorities for data determined almost entirely by the sponsoring agency. They point to the cases where decisions are established in competition with other program priorities within that department rather than with the statistical programs in other parts of the government. Others concentrate their criticism on the inefficiencies permeating a system that can sponsor at the same time a Consumer Expenditure Survey designed to represent the expenditures of all the country's consumers, a survey designed to secure detailed information on patient's expenditures on health services, and a survey designed to collect information on food use. Integration of all three into a single survey program could reduce cost and respondent burden while at the same time improving the analytical integration of the data collected.

An even more serious problem is that the national accounts are produced from data developed in many places with different concepts, time periods, and even different classification structures. Some point out that price indexes for deflation and for indexation may not be based on concepts appropriate for the uses made of them and that the samples developed for the collection of producer and consumer prices cannot be directly related to the relevant sales data, which are produced in a different statistical agency.

In the crucial area of education, data on outcomes from school-based surveys cannot always be combined statistically with data from employer-based surveys. More than a dozen government agencies collect or sponsor surveys that provide data on children, but researchers on the condition of children find many of the important pieces of information required for policy analysis missing. The National Center for Health Statistics sponsors the Health Interview Survey, but other parts of its parent department fund surveys which provide other pieces of information needed, and the pieces frequently cannot be put together very well.

The problem is in part budget, but in part also bureaucracy. Agencies tend to think in their own areas; they respond to the pressures placed upon them by their own policy analysts. Under these circumstances, it is difficult to take the broad view—especially when the OMB authority responsible for the coordination is without the resources to accomplish it.

The result is that very little effort is being made to integrate the wide variety of data sets produced by separate agencies into coherent subject-matter systems. Data collected in surveys conducted by one agency cannot easily be integrated with those collected by another. Although statistical agencies collect or sponsor many surveys, researchers often find data needed for analysis of important national problems missing.

Criticizing the system is easy. Fixing it is hard, and some of the criticisms have more validity than others. The federal statistical system *has* been slow to adjust to the changing economic conditions that it tries to measure. And it is true that federal statistics have not kept up with the shift from an economy with major emphasis on the production of goods to an economy producing services. But as the *Economist* described it, "Unlike things you can drop on your toe, a unit of output in services is tricky to define and difficult to measure; and it is even harder to take account of its improving quality" (September 11, 1993, p. 65). The output of a service-producing establishment is harder to count than factory production, and it is far more difficult to collect data from thousands of small establishments representing large numbers of small employers producing services, than it is from a few hundred large factories which produce most of the output of an entire industry. But it is also true that statistical agencies have responded to the challenge in different ways, a situation quite typical of a decentralized system.

However, there is a fundamental point to the complaints that underlies many of the perceived problems. A survey cannot be implemented, after all, unless the information to be collected is clearly defined and fully understood by those who respond to the questionnaires. This problem becomes extraordinarily complicated when we measure social and economic phenomena because disagreement exists about the values upon which the definitions rest. Although we do have statistical measures in a number of these difficult areas, for example, we do not have full agreement on what constitutes poverty, how to measure economic hardship, income adequacy, or medical care, or how to adjust measures for the constantly changing quality of products, especially those from the high technology industries. The national debate on health care, for example, has exposed serious deficiencies in our data system. We have a number of official surveys that measure the health of the American people, but these data are frequently difficult to integrate effectively with the large data base of administrative records that result from government health care programs.

Many cannot understand why the government, which spends more than a billion dollars to produce statistical products, does not always have the data it needs to inform public policy. Part of the problem is that economic and social conditions change rapidly, and the statistical indicators reflecting those conditions need to be regularly updated. Although the budget retrenchment of the early 1980s forced postponement of needed research and delayed the introduction of new technology, a number of steps have been taken during the last few years to move the improvement process along—especially for such major operations as the Current Population Survey, the Survey of Income and Program Participation, and the National Income and Product Accounts. The United States has also provided leadership in the international effort to move the national accounts of United Nations members to a unified system. This will make comparability among the countries of the world easier. Equally important, however, is the improvement the effort will bring to our own system of national accounts.

This is a time when we can profitably put our efforts into improving the government system which produces the data we criticize. In recent years, the use of statistical information in public policy decision making has increased markedly. At the same time, the policy issues themselves have become more complex and much more difficult to define. Controversial issues of public policy frequently feed discussion that cuts across the usual subject matter areas. Often the very definition of an issue comes from the statistical series that are available. That information then determines the route for the debate. Thus, the existence of statistical data about an issue of public policy and the availability of clear, understandable analyses based on the integration of data from diverse sources have become a necessity for effective decision making.

As a result, our need for better data is greater now than it was in the past. If we are to produce the data required for public policy, we need to ensure that the federal statistical system can produce the data in an environment that is efficient, modern, and open to change. A number of other countries have already recognized this need. The statistical systems of many of our major trading partners are better organized and better funded than ours. And the European Union (EU) recently began a major well-financed effort to develop modern statistics for EU integration. It is becoming increasingly difficult for this country to compete in a world where countries have more efficient organizations for producing statistics than we do and where they place a higher value on data development.

Notes

1. For example, the trade-off in resources allocated to the collection of data on the nation's farm population (who represent a small and declining proportion of the economy) and the workers and employers in the service-producing sector, a steadily enlarging sector.

Chapter Two

PAST IS PROLOGUE: WILL THE ISSUES EVER CHANGE?

The U.S. statistical system really began in 1860, with the establishment of the first statistical bureau in the Treasury Department, following the Pratt Commission's 1844 recommendation. Since then it has grown as government activity has expanded and the need for statistics relevant to new program areas has been recognized (see table 2.1). But as the government's statistical activity has expanded and new statistical bureaus have been created, little sustained attention has been given to methods either for ensuring the evaluation of overall priorities for data development or for determining quality standards across the widely decentralized system. Over the years a number of Commissions have reviewed organizational or data problems in the system. Most have done very good work. But the interest that generated establishment of each Commission was typically not sustained long enough to see that the recommendations were put into effect. Table 2.2 later in this chapter lists these Commissions and summarizes their recommendations and resulting action, if any.

Changes to the system did occur when the data requirements were recognized during World War I, when New Deal programs designed to cope with the Great Depression of the 1930s required data for implementation, and when statistical intelligence needed to carry on World War II expanded. Over those years, the government strove for greater coordination, but no sustained action to implement recommendations for more fundamental changes in the system ever took place. In those earlier years, as now, whenever cost overruns, data unavailability, or quality deterioration stimulated public concern, a new Commission was established to study the system again. But when its work was finished and its recommendations released, it would fade into oblivion, having brought about little change.

Table 2.1. OVERVIEW OF THE FEDERAL STATISTICAL SYSTEM 1860-1995

Date	Current Department	Current Statistical Agency	Antecedent or Previous History
1860-1880	Treasury	Statistics of Income Division (SOI)	Statistical Bureau created by law 1866; in Department of Commerce and Labor 1903; in Treasury 1913
	Agriculture	Economic Research Service (ERS)	Data and research provided for in Agriculture Department enabling act 1867
		National Agricultural Statistical Service (NASS)	Statistical research and analysis provided for in department enabling act 1867
	Education	National Center for Educational Statistics (NCES)	Statistics on condition and progress of education established in Department of Education by law 1867; broadened role in Department of Education 1979
1880-1900	Labor	Bureau of Labor Statistics (BLS)	Created as Bureau of Labor in Department of Interior by law 1884; independent agency acted as Department of Labor without executive rank; became Bureau in Department of Commerce and Labor 1903; part of Department of Labor 1913
1900-1920	Commerce	Bureau of the Census (Census)	Decennial Census required by Constitution; Permanent Bureau with expanded mission created 1902; in Department of Commerce and Labor; part of Department of Commerce 1913
	Health and Human Services	National Center for Health Statistics (NCHS)	Health data a concern of Public Health Service as early as 1912; Department of Health, Education and Welfare; Department of Health and Human Services 1980

Table 2.1. OVERVIEW OF THE FEDERAL STATISTICAL SYSTEM 1860-1995
        (Continued)

Date	Current Department	Current Statistical Agency	Antecedent or Previous History
1920-1940	Office of Management and Budget (OMB)	Statistical Policy Branch (SPB)	Committee on Government Statistics and Information Services 1933, then Central Statistical Board; Division of Statistical Standards in Bureau of Budget 1939–40; Office of Management and Budget 1970;. Transferred to Commerce Department 1987. Returned to OMB 1980 as Branch in Office of Regulatory and Information Affairs (OIRA)
1940-1960			
1960-1980	Energy	Energy Information Agency (EIA)	Created by law 1977 in new Department of Energy which consolidated energy activities
	Justice	Bureau of Justice Statistics (BJS)	Direct antecedent was Law Enforcement Assistance Administration. BJS in Justice System Improvement Act of 1979
1980-1995	Transportation	Bureau of Transportation Statistics (BTS)	Created by Intermodal Surface Transporation Efficiency Act 1991

THE DEPARTMENT OF COMMERCE AND LABOR

An opportunity to consolidate federal statistical work occurred in 1903, when Treasury's Division of Statistics was transferred to the newly created Department of Commerce and Labor, which already housed the Bureau of the Census and the Bureau of Labor [Statistics]. The opportunity was missed, however, when an interdepartmental committee proposed establishment of a committee to coordinate statistical activity but recommended against merging Treasury's Division of Statistics with the Bureau of the Census (Anderson 1988; p. 122; Committee on Statistical Reorganization 1908). Concentration of the power to conduct statistical inquiries in one place in the government, it was feared, would diminish the effectiveness of other agencies and create a statistical bureaucracy that might become more powerful than several other existing agencies.

THE BUREAU OF EFFICIENCY

The need for statistical information to pursue World War I renewed interest in the federal statistical system. In 1919, Congress asked the Bureau of Efficiency to review the duplication of statistical work, methods used for compiling government statistics, and scope of data required by the federal government. The Bureau of Efficiency, not a statistical agency itself, made the first detailed review of federal statistics compilation and in 1922 issued a report urging centralization of the statistical agencies then housed in some half dozen different departments. The Bureau recommended concentration of all non-administrative statistics in a central bureau in order to ease user access to data, to reduce survey burden, and to reduce costs. But decentralization, once begun, is hard to reverse. In addition to creation of separate agency bureaucracies, decentralization results in a series of stakeholder groups, each with a special interest in maintaining a particular part of the system. The Bureau's Report was referred to the Advisory Committee on the Census, which, after consideration, recommended no action to centralize the system.

THE COMMITTEE ON GOVERNMENT STATISTICS AND INFORMATION SERVICES

More efforts at coordination occurred in the early 1930s when the Committee on Government Statistics and Information Services (COGSIS), formed under the auspices of the American Statistical Association and the Social Science Research Council, studied the statistical needs of New Deal legislation. COGSIS recommended greater coordination, reviewed statistical methodology for a number of important government statistical series, and discussed the staffing and funding of statistical units within the various departments or agencies (Social Science Research Council 1937). During the deliberations of COGSIS in 1934 and 1935, many recognized the need for statistical data for much of the New Deal program, but the new government agencies generally wanted to develop their own statistical groups. Others, however, felt that it would not be possible for such programmatic agencies to develop objective data. COGSIS voted for continued decentralization of the system but argued that much stronger coordination was needed. It recommended expansion of the power of the recently established Central Statistical Board. The Central Statistical Board took on the recommended additional authority and, in fact, much of the later development of government statistics occurred under the Board's leadership. The Board's functions were transferred to the Bureau of the Budget in 1939 and were further strengthened in 1942 and 1950.

THE MILLS-LONG REPORT

A generation later, in 1948, as a part of the study of government organization, the Hoover Commission asked the National Bureau of Economic Research to undertake a study of the statistical system. The NBER report, written by F. C. Mills and Clarence Long, commented on the problems of resource allocation, data comparability, variation in data quality from one producing agency to another, and focused on the lack of coordination within the system (Mills and Long 1940). The Mills-Long report generally supported the decentralized structure of the Federal statistical system but recommended that large-scale, repetitive surveys be centralized in the Bureau of the Census. The report also proposed an independent Office of Statistical Standards and Services within the Executive Office of the President with a presidentially-appointed head, and pointed to the lack of comparability of data collected from different sources, commented on the variation in data quality, and expressed concern about the burden placed by government on survey respondents. Their report criticized the lack of coordination in budgeting practices for statistics, both in the Executive Branch and in Congress, where as many as nine separate subcommittees in each house of Congress had to pass on parts of the statistical-agency budgets. The Hoover Commission, which considered the Mills-Long report, supported many of the report's recommendations but believed the Office of Statistical Standards should continue to be located in the Bureau of the Budget. The Commission recommended greater use of the Census Bureau, but not centralization of large-scale surveys in it. Thus, in accordance with the well-established pattern for recommendations about the statistical system, no action was taken to centralize public use statistics or to reform the budget process.

THE KAYSEN COMMITTEE

Nearly 20 years passed before another serious attempt to review the federal statistical system took place. In 1966, the then Bureau of the Budget established the Kaysen Committee to examine storage of and access to government statistics. The Committee soon determined, however, that it could only consider the questions put to it in the context of organization of the statistical system as a whole. Impressed with the inefficiencies and duplication within the system, the committee recommended that nonadministrative statistics should gradually be centralized and that a National Data Center be established as a first step toward that goal. Because of the importance of coordination to the proposed data center, the Kaysen Committee recommended appointment of a new Director of the Federal Statistical System in the Executive Office of the president, who would supervise coordination of the system and the National Data Center. The Committee also recommended moving the Census Bureau out of the Commerce Department and placing it under the direction of the new Director of the Federal Statistical System (Report 1966). None of these recommendations were implemented.

THE WALLIS COMMISSION

The Wallis Commission, established by President Nixon in 1971, had a somewhat more lasting effect. Headed by Allan Wallis as chair and Frederick Mosteller as vice-chair, the commission focused on practical methods "to strengthen the system's capacity for self-improvement and self-renewal" (Wallis letter to Nixon, Report 1971). Recognizing that the statistical system would always find it hard to produce data needed for public policy on a timely basis, the commission said that "the convulsive nature of political events rules out orderly specification of statistical requirements and ensures tardy adjustment to kaleidoscopic changes" (Report 1971, p.1). Nevertheless, the Commission recommended a series of changes designed to a) broaden the scope of coordinating and auditing activities by OMB's Statistical ✓

Policy Division and a newly created Advisory Group as a part of the National Research Council at the National Academy of Sciences; b) develop systematic efforts to eliminate obsolete statistical programs; c) increase public confidence in national statistics; and d) develop more integration in data collection to increase the comparability of economic statistics.

To carry out these general principles, the commission made a number of specific recommendations. The most lasting recommended creation of the Committee on National Statistics (CNSTAT), which recently celebrated its 20th anniversary. The CNSTAT, to function under the National Research Council at the National Academy of Sciences, was envisaged by the Commission as the evaluation advisor to OMB on statistical programs. The Wallis Commission emphasized the need for a regular program of evaluation of existing statistical programs, and proposed that every budget proposal for a new statistical program contain an evaluation component. Although CNSTAT has had a number of important successes in evaluating a series of important statistical programs, it has operated only as an advisor to the statistical agencies themselves or occasionally to a Congressional committee, not as an evaluation advisor to OMB as the Wallis Commission had intended. Indeed, in a move to reduce the involvement of OMB, the coordination of contributions from the statistical agencies to the funding of a small basic staff for CNSTAT, which had originally been an OMB responsibility, was transferred to the National Research Council at the National Academy of Sciences. CNSTAT studies have proved to be relatively expensive (even though the CNSTAT members and panel members serve without compensation), and only the agencies with the largest budgets have been able to commission CNSTAT evaluations of their work.

The Wallis Commission's emphasis on evaluation studies was important, and both Congress and the statistical agencies have benefited. But the recommendation was only partly implemented, since the CNSTAT does not have the special advisory role with OMB as originally intended. A good deal of attention, through interagency discussion, was given to the Wallis Commission recommendation for legislation to permit the transfer of confidential microdata between statistical agencies for statistical purposes, but no action was taken on the request. It took some 20 years before such an approach was approved by the president (in the FY 1992 budget), but no specific legislative action was taken by Congress. The recommendation for the Census Bureau to create and maintain an industrial directory (or list of business establishments) for data collection purposes was funded in accordance with the Wallis Commission recommendation. But the list was never shared with the other agencies, making it impossible to use it to improve surveys throughout the system. This issue is currently being reconsidered under the leadership of OMB's statistical policy group, which is working with the National Agricultural Statistical Service and the Bureau of Labor Statistics to develop a business list which could (with proper safeguards to protect confidentiality) be made available to the system as a whole for data collection purposes.

Attention has also been given, especially in recent years, to the confidentiality pledge in data collection activities and clarification of reporting requirements placed on respondents by the government. But the independent Advisory Board recommended by the Wallis Commission to review the protection of privacy and confidentiality by federal government collection agencies has never been established.

THE MALKIEL SUBCOMMITTEE

By the mid-1970s, therefore, the federal statistical system had been considered—and reconsidered—several times. Recommendations to improve coordination of the system, to increase comparability of data, to enhance the protection of confidentiality, and to improve methods of budgeting had been made, considered, and, for the most part, not acted upon.

It was at that time, largely as the result of the efforts of Julius Shiskin, then Commissioner of Labor Statistics but formerly Chief of OMB's statistical policy group, that the President's Council of Economic Advisors (CEA) began more direct involvement in federal statistics. The Subcommittee on Economic Statistics, a subgroup of the cabinet-level Economic Policy Board, was established under CEA leadership, with membership from the major cabinet agencies which had statistical agencies dealing with economic statistics. The group, serving as advisors to the Office of Management and Budget and the President, focused its attention on coordination of budget proposals and a review of program needs for economic statistics. As part of this effort, questions were raised about organizational issues and the cost of duplication within the system.

The first subcommittee was chaired by Burton Malkiel, a member of the Council. Although noting that the federal statistical system was too fragmented (there being some 108 separate agencies collecting some kind of statistical data at the time), the subcommittee could not agree on the optimal degree of centralization within the system. Instead, the subcommittee recommended that statistical data gathering should be consolidated in up to 10 agencies, on the argument that efficiency as well as improved methodology would result from the creation of certified statistical collection centers, which could be assigned new statistical functions as needed. The subcommittee also discussed the need to strengthen the Statistical Policy Division of OMB, as well as possible establishment of a Committee of Outside Advisers, to provide input on broad issues of statistical policy and to assist in preservation of the system's integrity. The subcommittee gave advice on program priorities, which proved useful during the budget process, but once again, little organizational change took place.

In the fall of 1977, however, there was some movement. The statistical policy function was transferred from OMB to the Department of Commerce, which had responsibility for the Bureau of the Census and the Bureau of Economic Analysis. The transfer, which turned out to be short-lived, carried out a part of the Kaysen Committee's recommendation but ignored a critical element in that recommendation—namely, that a Chief Statistician's office be created in the Executive Office of the president with responsibility for the coordination activity as well as for the Bureau of the Census, and a newly created National Data Center. The new location did nothing to enhance the prestige of the Director of the Statistical Policy Division. In fact, it made the task of coordinating the system more difficult than ever.

JOINT AD HOC COMMITTEE ON GOVERNMENT STATISTICS

As a result of the growing concerns over problems of coordinating the federal statistical system, a Joint Ad Hoc Committee on Government Statistics met to examine the state of the system and its data. Members of the Committee represented the major professional associations interested in government statistics: American Sociological Association, American Statistical Association, Federal Statistics Users' Conference, National Association of Business Economists, and the Population Association of America. The American Public Health Association nominated a representative to serve as liason with the Committee. The Ad Hoc Committee considered coordination of statistical activities; analysis, access and dissemination of data; analytical needs; advisory committees; and the use of statistics in legislation.

Because the Committee did not have time to study each of these issues carefully, it made several general recommendations. Of particular importance was their recognition that the resources for planning and coordination were inadequate for the increasing complexity of the federal government's data system. Coordination should be strengthened, the Committee said, both among the statistical agencies themselves and on statistical issues between the executive and legislative branches of government as well as among federal, state, and local levels of government. Rather than decide on a strengthened statistical policy function or creation of a more centralized authority, the Ad Hoc Committee suggested ". . . a thorough review of the major subjects" it had identified, mentioning cooperation in such a study by the Committee on National Statistics of the National Research Council (Statistical Reporter, September 1976).

THE ECKLER-MILLS REPORT

At about this time, CNSTAT, referred to earlier as established as the result of a Wallis Commission recommendation, commissioned a study of the federal statistical system. The study—by A. Ross Eckler, former Census Director, and Thomas J. Mills—was undertaken because CNSTAT had been asked to consider the planning and coordination of government statistics by the Joint Ad Hoc Committee on Government Statistics.

Pointing to the reduced staff of the Statistical Policy Division and to the general downgrading of the coordination function which had occurred since the end of World War II, Eckler and Mills (*Statistical Reporter*, August 1978) reviewed once again the organizational problems of the federal statistical system, emphasized the need for change, and laid out a series of possibilities ranging from a strengthened coordinating group to full centralization of the system.

THE BONNEN PROJECT

At just about this time, in the fall of 1977, the organization of the federal statistical system received attention at a higher level of the executive branch. The White House asked Professor James T. Bonnen of Michigan State University to head a President's Reorganization

Project for the Federal Statistical System. Professor Bonnen began work early in 1978, with assistance from representatives of the Departments of Commerce, Agriculture, Labor, Health, Education and Welfare, the National Science Foundation, and the National Aeronautics and Space Administration. Ivan Fellegi, then Assistant Chief Statistician on leave from Statistics Canada, also participated in the project.

The Bonnen project focused on five major areas: 1) the perceived lack of policy relevance of data produced by the system; 2) periodic threats to the integrity of data; 3) inadequate quality; 4) inadequate protection of the privacy of respondents; and 5) excessive paperwork. Each of these issues had been considered before, although not in so comprehensive a manner. But some changes had occurred since the earlier reviews. As mentioned above, in October 1977, the coordination function previously located in the Office of Management and Budget (formerly the Bureau of the Budget) was transferred to the Department of Commerce, in a new Office of Federal Statistical Policy and Standards (OFSPS). The transfer was made as a temporary move pending the outcome of a comprehensive study of the issue by the President's Reorganization Project.

The Reorganization Project recommended establishment of an enlarged Office of Statistical Policy in the Executive Office of the President, with responsibility for the coordination of data required for public policy and for managing the Federal Statistical System (see President's Reorganization Project 1980). The Office of Statistical Policy was to have responsibility for program planning, review and clearance of statistical forms, burden control, analysis and integration, user services, statistical standards, and fair information practices. In addition, Bonnen proposed uniform legislative provisions for protection of confidentiality, for exchange of microdata for statistical purposes between statistical agencies, and for development of the Standard Statistical Establishment List for use in survey sampling.

The Bonnen project was the first of all the studies of the federal statistical system to result in a presidential-level recommendation for reorganization. Its report was perhaps the most comprehensive and ambitious examination of the problems of the U.S. statistical system yet undertaken. The Administration submitted legislation incorporating many of the recommendations of the project—most importantly, that an office to carry out the Bonnen project recommendations for statistical analysis, coordination, and database functions under the leadership of a presidentially-appointed Chief Statistician be established in the Executive Office of the President.[1] Unfortunately, the recommendation came so close to the end of the Carter Administration that no action was taken by Congress. In any case, Congress had just passed the Paperwork Reduction Act, which combined the respondent burden imposed by regulatory agencies with the respondent burden for general-purpose statistics into one goal for burden reduction and moved the Statistical Policy Division out of Commerce and back to OMB. Rather than strengthening the coordination of statistics, however, the Act further weakened the Division's authority by placing it within the Office of Information and Regulatory Affairs. Instead of elevating the chief of the Statistical Policy Division (SPD) as Bonnen had proposed, the law reduced the importance of that official within the OMB hierarchy. It is unlikely that Congress would have considered reversing its new stand in this area.[2] In any case, the Reagan Administration came into office and took no action on the Bonnen project recommendations, focusing its attention on reducing the regulatory burden.

The federal statistical system deteriorated still further in the early days of the Reagan Administration. The staff of the Statistical Policy Branch was cut drastically, and the entire focus of attention shifted away from the improvement of statistical quality. As across-the-board budget reductions were legislated for many government agencies, a number of data programs were reduced or eliminated. The budget in each of the major statistical agencies was cut, with little organized review of the effects of those cuts on the data produced by the other statistical agencies. These actions pointed out once again the difficulties that can occur in a decentralized system with weak coordination, as well as in a system where the coordination authority focuses more on budget reduction than on statistics production.

THE REAGAN PERIOD

The organization of the federal statistical system was an issue discussed within the Reagan Administration on several occasions, despite lack of constructive action. The former Director of the Bureau of the Census, Bruce Chapman, unsuccessfully proposed consolidation of agencies in June 1985 in a memorandum to Mr. Meese, then a senior official in the White House.

Later, when the Reagan Administration put forward proposals to reorganize the Commerce Department to increase efficiency, the statistical organizational issue arose once again. In order to make the proposed reorganization more palatable to Congress, the Secretary of Commerce wanted to reduce the size of the new Department and suggested that a new home be found for the Census Bureau with its sizable staff. Consideration was first given to moving Census to the Treasury Department. Since the Census Bureau served as the nation's primary survey collector of confidential income data, it seemed unwise to place it in the Treasury Department, which served as the nation's tax collector. Although it was not publicly known, consideration at this time was given to the possibility of combining the Bureau of the Census with the Bureau of Labor Statistics in the Department of Labor. The thought was that the demographic work of the Census Bureau fit readily into the responsibilities of the Labor Department, and that the economic work of the Census Bureau could be done at Labor as well. Some at OMB hoped that such a combination could, in the long run, improve the quality of the data produced by both agencies while at the same time reducing cost through the reduction of perceived duplication of data collection. Secretary of Labor Raymond Donovan considered this suggestion (it had not yet become a serious proposal) but pointed to concerns that were developing over the high cost of the population census and the problems of enumerating the entire population. While the issue was alive enough for discussion between OMB and the Secretary of Labor—and at the Labor Department among the Secretary, the Undersecretary, and the Commissioner of Labor Statistics—it was dropped before it went any further. Congress took no action on the Commerce reorganization legislation, and the Census Bureau remained in the Department of Commerce.

Statistical policy coordination continued to deteriorate during the Reagan Administration as OMB concentrated on the regulation reduction portion of the Office of Information and Regulatory Affairs in which the Statistical Policy Division was now located. Personnel in the Office were reassigned, so that only a skeleton staff remained for statistical coordination. The then Director of Statistical Policy considered budget and respondent burden reduction to be the main tasks of the Division.

THE BOSKIN WORKING GROUP

When the Bush Administration came into office, the new Chairman of the Council of Economic Advisors, Michael Boskin, heeding the growing concerns of the economics and statistics professions about the nation's data system, established a Working Group on Statistics which he himself chaired. The Working Group concentrated initially on programmatic and budget issues but soon found itself faced with the age-old issue of statistical organization. A subcommittee of the Working Group was charged with looking into the possible elimination of duplication, determination of cost savings, or improvements in quality that might result from a change in the organization of the statistical system. The subcommittee reviewed much of the ground that had been covered in previous reviews of the U.S. system and added yet another review of the systems in place in other countries. The atmosphere this time around was quite different from before. Many of the statistical agencies had suffered budget reductions during the Reagan years, the difficult-to-measure service-producing sector of the economy was growing, and response to the decennial Census mailing was considerably lower than in the past. Many of the senior office chiefs in the large statistical agencies, rather than opposing change because of turf worries, had expressed the view that consolidation of at least the four largest agencies—Census, BLS, National Agricultural Statistical Service, and Bureau of Economic Analysis—would help to shore up the system.

Nevertheless, the Working Group decided against any organizational change. One reason was that any savings from consolidation, especially during the early years, would not be large and could be secured from legislation to change confidentiality laws to permit the sharing of data between agencies for statistical purposes. They were also concerned that the political problems involved in organizational change could be time-consuming, traumatic and costly.

Instead, the Boskin Working Group concentrated on program enhancement primarily through budget increases, recommended that the President request "sharing" legislation, and suggested once again that OMB consider development of one or more business establishment lists that could be used by all the agencies in the system. The President's budget for 1991 and later years reflected the Working Group's priorities and requested increases for statistical programs. The President's budget message for that year also included reference to the submission of new "sharing" legislation. In addition, funds were added to develop a Center for Statistical Survey Education in the Washington, D.C. area to train people who work in statistical agencies.

*   *   *

Table 2.2. COMMITTEES, COMMISSIONS AND STUDY GROUPS: 1903-1990

Date	Name	Recommendations (and their fate)
1903	Commission appointed by Secretary of Treasury	For some consolidation of statistical units but against centralization. **No action taken.**
1908	Commission appointed by Secretary of Commerce and Labor	Against consolidation of Census and Bureau of Statistics (formerly of Treasury); in favor of establishing a coordinating committee. **Committee established, but did nothing.**
1922	Bureau of Efficiency	For centralized Bureau of Statistics to increase efficiency. **Report referred to Advisory Committee on Census which opted against centralization.**
1933	Committee on Government Statistics and Information Services (COGSIS) established by American Statistical Association and Social Science Research Association	For continuation of decentralized system but expanding Central Statistical Board power to coordinate statistics—to advise but not control action. **Central Statistical Board in 1940 converted into Division of Statistical Standards in Bureau of the Budget (now Office of Management and Budget OMB).**
1948	Mills-Long Report for Hoover Commission	For centralizing repetitive, large-scale surveys in Census Bureau, otherwise continuing system as it was, and establishing independent Office of Statistical Standards (OSS) in Executive Office of President with Presidentially appointed head. **OSS left in Bureau of the Budget. No action taken to centralize large scale surveys in the Census Bureau.**
1955	Internal Bureau of Budget review of Mills-Long recommendations	Pointed out problems of centralization. No action taken.
1966	Kaysen Committee established by Bureau of the Budget	For gradual centralization of non-administrative statistics and establishment of National Data Center. Recommended new Director of the Federal Statistical System in the Executive Office of the President to coordinate the system and the National Data Center. Proposed moving the Census Bureau from the Department of Commerce to the Executive Office of the President, to function under the new Director of the Federal Statistical System. **Recommendations not implemented.**

Table 2.2. COMMITTEES, COMMISSIONS AND STUDY GROUPS: 1903-1990
(Continued)

Date	Name	Recommendations (and their fate)
1971	Wallis Commission established by President Nixon	For broadening the scope of coordination, and establishing a system of auditing, and establishing Committee on National Statistics (CNSTAT) at the National Research Council to advise OMB. **CNSTAT established. Develops reviews for advice to individual agencies but has not been used as an advisor to OMB.**
1970s	Subcommittee of the Council of Economic Advisors chaired by Burton Malkiel	For centralization but no agreement on degree. Finally suggested centralization into 10 statistical agencies and strengthening Office of Statistical Policy. Recommended appointment of Committee of Outside Advisors. **No action taken.**
1971	President's Departmental Reorganization Proposals	For consolidating federal domestic functions into four new Departments, in particular, a new Department of Economic Affairs to include the Bureau of Economic Analysis, Census Bureau, Bureau of Labor Statistics, National Agricultural Statistical Service, Economic Research Service from the statistical system and several other scientific organizations. **Submitted to Congress but no action taken.**
1976	Joint Ad Hoc Committee on Government Statistics	For strengthening coordination or moving toward centralization. Recommended further study in cooperation with CNSTAT. CNSTAT commissioned Report
1976	Eckler-Mills Report for Committee on National Statistics	For more centralization and better coordination. **No action taken.**
1977	President's Reorganization Project headed by James Bonnen. Followed congressional action eliminating Office of Statistical Policy from OMB and placing part of its responsibilities in the Department of Commerce.	For establishment of an enlarged Office of Statistical Policy with enhanced status and responsibilities in the Executive Office of the President. **Plan submitted to Congress at end of Carter Administration. No action taken.**

Table 2.2. COMMITTEES, COMMISSIONS AND STUDY GROUPS: 1903-1990
(Continued)

Date	Name	Recommendations (and their fate)
1980	Paperwork Reduction Act	Passed, Transferred Statistical Policy back to OMB but as part of Office of Information and Regulatory Affairs (OIRA). Statistical Policy became a branch in OIRA.
1985	Bruce Chapman proposal to Edwin Meese with request that it be forwarded to Cabinet Council for Domestic Policy. Chapman and Meese both on White House staff.	For consolidation of Statistical Policy of eight agencies—Census, BEA, BLS,NASS, EIA,NCHS, NCES, and BJS—into a new U.S. Statistics Agency, USSA. All OMB statistical policy functions to be merged with the office of U.S. Statistics Agency. Administrator, an Executive Level II official appointed by President with consent of Senate. Establishment of a Statistical Advisory Board of Government officials to represent interests of the departments; Board would be advisory to USSA, but could send advice to President independently of USSA. **No action taken.**
1990	Working Group of the Cabinet Council for Economic Policy, chaired by Michael Boskin, Chairman of Council of Economic Affairs	Against consolidation; savings would be small and change not considered worth the cost in disruption.

As this brief history indicates, in spite of a long series of studies of the federal statistical system conducted over the last 150 years, the system has changed very little. New agencies have been continually created to meet new data needs as new fields emerged as national priorities, with little attention to the data collection activities already underway. Concerns about data comparability, international statistical activity, budget retrenchment, respondent burden, data quality, and the adequacy of data for public policy have waxed and waned over time, with a concomitant waxing and waning of coordination efforts. But action to effectuate lasting change has faltered through lack of budgetary and popular support for statistics in general, bureaucratic inertia, and fear of unleashing opposition from the large number of stake-holders with a special interest in retaining strong, relatively independent agencies within the particular subject matter departments.

Each of the reviews has had a somewhat different emphasis, reflecting the atmosphere in which the review took place. But almost every study that has taken place since 1844 has given attention to centralization vs. decentralization, decision-making vs. advisory power for the coordination authority, placement of the coordination office within the overall government structure, reduction of survey burden, creation of a centralized database for easier user access, and protection of confidentiality. Neither the issues themselves nor the proposed solutions have changed very much over the last century and a half.

The record shows that this country has failed to develop sustained interest in statistical information. Particular problems of data revision, data concept, or data quality hit the public spotlight on occasion, but the public interest quickly reverts to other issues thought to affect policy more directly. Is the situation different today? Perhaps so. The news media have become convinced that the statistical system has not kept up with the changing economy. The professional community is ever more concerned about the quality and the coverage of the data produced, in particular about the shrinking survey response rates that reflect the U.S. public's growing distrust of government and concern about protection of privacy. Congress is trying to have it both ways. It is focusing attention increasingly on the high cost of data gathering at the same time as it is highlighting the insufficiency of the databases needed in such important policy areas as health care, education, and the protection of the environment.

Notes

1. Bonnen proposed a much larger staff for coordination than the recommendation that was sent forward.

2. Bonnen tried to reach agreement with the congressional committee considering the Paperwork Reduction Act but was unsuccessful.

Chapter Three

THE FEDERAL STATISTICAL SYSTEM: IS DECENTRALIZATION FRAGMENTATION?

The American statistical system is surely one of the most decentralized data-producing systems in the world. It includes agencies whose basic mission is to produce and analyze statistical data located in a number of different government departments. In addition, a large number of other agencies (in a multitude of government departments) produce administrative, survey, or evaluation statistics as part of their programmatic responsibilities. As new pressures to produce the information required for public policy have developed, some Cabinet agencies have created new statistical divisions.[1] Although most other countries have moved toward centralization of statistical work in a single agency of the government, the United States has moved in the opposite direction, creating more and more separate statistical functions throughout government. These moves have increased concerns about the problems of coordination of statistical activities, duplication of effort among the statistical agencies, as well as other inefficiencies that these organizational arrangements may have spawned.

Even when narrowly defined, the federal statistical system includes nearly a dozen agencies located in nine government departments. The 11 formal statistical agencies of the United States government have a combined annual budget of more than $1 billion (excluding the cost of the decennial census), dealing with an extraordinary array of public policy issues (table 3.1). In addition to the formal statistical agencies, a large number of other federal government units produce statistics from surveys and other special purpose data collection activities for use in program implementation and evaluation. These bring the budget expenditures for federal statistics collection to a much higher level. The OMB lists more than 70 individual agencies with annual budgets of $500,000 or more for statistical activities, and estimates that the government's FY 1994 budget requests for statistical operations total about $2.7 billion.[2]

Table 3.1. FY 1995 CONGRESSIONAL APPROPRIATIONS FOR STATISTICAL
AGENCIES (in millions of dollars)

Bureau of Labor Statistics[a]	352.9
Bureau of the Census[b]	278.1
National Center for Educational Statistics[c]	90.8
Energy Information Administration	84.7
National Center for Health Statistics[d]	81.5
National Agricultural Statistical Service	81.4
Economic Research Service	53.9
Bureau of Economic Analysis	42.2
Statistics of Income Division, IRS	25.1
Bureau of Justice Statistics	24.1
Bureau of Transportation Statistics	15.0
TOTAL: 11 Agencies	$1,171.7

a. Includes $50.2 million from Trust Funds.
b. Includes $142.1 from Current Salaries and Expenses budget as well as $136.0 from
Periodic budget. The 1995 work on the 2000 Census is funded at about $42 million.
c. Includes $65.0 million for National Assessment and $60.0 million for other statistics.
d. Includes PHS evaluation funds which represent a significant part of the total.
Source: Coalition of Professional Associations for Federal Statistics.

All this work is loosely coordinated by a small group of people[3] located in the Office of Information and Regulatory Affairs in the Office of Management and Budget. OMB's Statistical Policy Branch (SPB) has policy oversight and coordinating responsibility for all of the government's statistical activities. SPB sets classification and quality standards, oversees the protection of objectivity and confidentiality, approves collection forms used in some government surveys, represents the country at the United Nations Statistical Commission, and coordinates all statistical activities of the government with those of other countries. Since the early 1930s, those interested in improving statistics in this country have tried to increase the size and the power of the SPB as key to moving the federal government's statistical system forward and improving the quality of data. Interest in strengthening the policy and coordinating arm of the system, however, (like the budgets for statistics in general) has risen and fallen with the state of the economy and with the public's awareness of the need for high quality public information.

The rest of the chapter reviews the functions of different pieces of the federal statistical system, beginning with the two large multipurpose statistical agencies. Table 3.2 provides a guide to the discussion.

Table 3.2. FEDERAL STATISTICAL AGENCIES: PLACEMENT WITHIN HOST DEPARTMENTS

A. Report directly to the Secretary:

   Bureau of Labor Statistics

   Energy Information Administration

   Bureau of Transportation Statistics

B. Report to the Secretary through an Assistant or Undersecretary (through one layer):

   Bureau of the Census—Undersecretary for Economic and Statistical Affairs

   National Center for Educational Statistics—Assistant Secretary for Education and Research

   Bureau of Economic Analysis—Undersecretary for Economic and Statistical Affairs

   National Agricultural Statistical Service—Assistant Secretary for Economic Affairs

   Economic Research Service, USDA—Assistant Secretary for Economic Affairs

C. Report to the Secretary through several layers:

   Bureau of Justice Statistics—Assistant Attorney General and Associate Attorney General

   National Center for Health Statistics—Director, Center for Disease Control and Surgeon General of Public Health

   Statistics of Income Division—Assistant Commissioner for Taxpayer Service and Returns Processing and Commissioner of Internal Revenue

CENSUS AND LABOR STATISTICS

The Bureau of the Census

Article 1, Section 2(3) of the U.S. Constitution mandates the use of statistical information in the operation of government, providing that a population census be conducted every decade to serve as the basis for reapportionment of the House of Representatives. For many years, the country had no permanent Census Bureau, with U.S. marshals conducting the earliest censuses in addition to their other duties. Later, statistical bureaus in state governments did the data collection, with a Superintendent of the Census in Washington overseeing the national requirements. In 1902, Congress created a permanent Bureau of the Census to compile the decennial Census and to collect and publish other large sets of general-purpose statistics. The legislative foundation for the Census Bureau specifically included legal protection for individual privacy and the confidentiality of the data collected from all respondents. Begun in the Department of the Interior, the

Census Bureau was transferred to the Department of Commerce and Labor in 1903. When Commerce was separated from Labor in 1913, the Census Bureau became a permanent part of the Department of Commerce. The law establishing the Census Bureau provides for a Director appointed by the President with the consent of the Senate; the Director serves at the pleasure of the President. Although not stated in the law, the Directorship has been treated as a political appointment, with its incumbent changing after each Presidential election.

The Census Bureau—in pursuit of its broad mandate to produce general-purpose statistics—collects, tabulates, and publishes a large amount of census and survey data, some as a part of its own mission and some on contract with other agencies of the government. In addition to the decennial censuses of population and housing, and quinquennial censuses of agriculture and business, the Census Bureau conducts surveys that provide information at more frequent intervals. These surveys are funded in part directly by the Census Bureau's current budget (FY 1995 appropriation was $136.0 million) and in part through contracts with other agencies like the Bureau of Labor Statistics and the National Center for Health Statistics (see further below).[4] The budget for the Census Bureau to continue analysis and dissemination of the 1990 decennial census data and conduct the Economic Census was $142.1 million. Census' total funding for FY 1994 amounted to $278.1 million. The 2000 census work in FY 1995 is funded at a $42.0 million level.

Organizationally, the Census Bureau is housed within the Economic and Statistics Administration of the Department of Commerce. Its Director reports to an Undersecretary whose statistical responsibilities include both the Bureau of Economic Analysis (which in turn has responsibility for the national income and product accounts) and Census's own statistical programs. Thus, the Director of the Census Bureau, a presidential appointee, reports to the Secretary and the Deputy Secretary of Commerce through an Undersecretary. Although the Bureau has asserted its independence and objectivity over the years, major issues of statistical policy are reviewed in the Undersecretary's office. In recent years especially, important Census Bureau decisions have been made by the Undersecretary and, as in the case of the decennial census, by the Secretary of Commerce.[5]

The decennial census, economic and agricultural censuses, and most of the other surveys of the Census Bureau are carried out under the authority granted by law as set forth in Title 13 of the U.S. Code. Statistical data compiled by the Census Bureau are rigorously protected by Title 13 to ensure that the identity of individuals is scrupulously protected. The laws have been interpreted restrictively by the Bureau, the Department, and the Courts, and, as a result, the microdata collected by the Bureau of the Census are generally not made available outside the Bureau.[6] Indeed, Census has maintained that Title 13 prohibits it from sharing its microdata with other agencies in the statistical system—even those that can demonstrate many years of successful protection of respondent confidentiality.

The work of the Bureau of the Census is dominated, even in the intercensal years, by its responsibility to carry out the decennial census of the population. This is a huge and expensive undertaking. The 1990 Census cost 2.6 billion dollars. It takes many years to plan and serves several crucial functions. It provides important information for use by the statistical system, for example, forms the sampling frame for all the government's household surveys, and provides the data on which large sums of money are distributed to states and localities. Even more important, census counts provide the data required for allocation of seats in the House of Representatives, application of the Voting Rights Act, and implementation of a series of other laws passed by the Congress.

In addition to its own programs of survey work, the Bureau of the Census provides the foundation for much of the demographic and economic information on which the nation's public and private decision making is based. It conducts household surveys for other parts of the statistical system, including surveys on health, crime, housing, and the labor force. And the economic side of the Census Bureau produces large amounts of information used by other agencies and departments of the government. The quinquennial economic census, for example, produces information used by the Bureau of Labor Statistics in its price and productivity programs and by the Bureau of Economic Analysis in compiling the national accounts.

The Bureau of Labor Statistics

With an FY 1995 budget of $352.9 million, the Bureau of Labor Statistics (BLS), located in the Department of Labor, is the second large anchor of the federal statistical system. BLS was created by the Congress in 1884 as the Bureau of Labor, with a mission to ". . . acquire and diffuse among the people of the United States useful information on subjects connected with labor . . . ". The founding legislation also provided that the Bureau concern itself with the relation of labor to capital, working hours, earnings and " . . . the means of promoting their [workers'] material, social, intellectual, and moral prosperity" (29 U.S. Code chapter 1, par. 1). To carry out its mission, BLS collects, compiles, analyzes, and disseminates information on employment and unemployment, prices and living conditions, wages and other worker compensation, industrial relations, productivity and technology, economic growth and employment projections, and occupational safety and health.

The current mission of BLS is a dual one. First, it is the statistical arm of the Labor Department and, as such, provides advice on statistical issues and analysis of data to other agencies within the Department and to the Secretary. But second, it is also an independent statistical agency in its own right. As such, it interacts directly with other executive branch agencies (especially the Federal Reserve Board and the Council of Economic Advisors), the Congress, and the public. Of course, the Census Bureau—and many of the other agencies discussed later in this chapter—also have direct interaction on data issues outside their individual departments. But there is an important difference.

The Commissioner of Labor Statistics, unlike the Director of the Census Bureau and many of the other statistical agency heads, although appointed by the President with consent of the Senate, does not serve at the pleasure of the President but has a four-year term of office. Reappointment to more than one term has become a tradition, providing the BLS with more continuity of leadership and considerable independence. Within the Department of Labor, the Commissioner reports directly to the Secretary, has the same rank as the other Assistant Secretary agency heads, participates directly in the Secretary's staff meetings, and confers on data analyses from time to time with the Assistant Secretaries and their programmatic Bureaus within the Department of Labor. As the agency releasing politically sensitive data each month on issues like unemployment and inflation, BLS has worked out special measures designed to ensure a public belief in its objectivity, accuracy, and independence from political control. Its releases are not cleared by the Labor Department, it handles most of its administration and personnel issues without Labor's involvement, and the Commissioner refrains from participating in any policy decisions.

Much of the BLS's success in developing and retaining its independence in managing its staff and resources has resulted from the stability and longevity of the terms of office of its heads. Since its creation in 1884, until the present—110 years—BLS has had only 11 Commissioners. Their average tenure has been far longer than the

Secretary of Labor and the Assistant Secretaries heading the other agencies within the Department. In fact, the Commissioner of Labor Statistics has had much longer tenure than any of the other statistical agency heads. The BLS has, therefore, had the sustained leadership necessary to develop and implement long-range plans, build a relationship of trust with the Congress and the public, and foster development of an objective and dedicated staff.[7]

EDUCATION, AGRICULTURE, ENERGY, AND HEALTH

National Center for Educational Statistics

The total NCES budget for FY 1995 amounts to a little more than $90 million, a congressional appropriation of $80.9 million plus $9.9 million from other Department of Education funds. The total NCES budget for FY 1995 amounts to a little more than $90 million.

In enacting legislation for the National Center for Educational Statistics, Congress built, in part, on the BLS model. The head of the Center is called a Commissioner, is appointed by the President with the consent of the Senate, and serves a four-year term of office. However, there are significant differences between the status of the National Center for Education Statistics within the Department of Education and that of the Bureau of Labor Statistics in the Department of Labor. NCES is not an administratively independent agency within its Department, with its own budget and appropriated personnel complement. Rather, the Office of Educational Research and Improvement (OERI), which is headed by an Assistant Secretary, has overall responsibility for the Statistics Center as well as for the program for educational research. The Commissioner of Education Statistics reports to that Assistant Secretary. As a result, the Commissioner of Educational Statistics is placed lower in the table of organization in Education than is the Commissioner of Labor Statistics in Labor. Moreover, the head of the National Center for Educational Statistics has neither the authority nor the independence of the Commissioner of Labor Statistics. In fact, in reviewing the education statistics budget requests, the Congress does not approve staffing levels as it does in reviewing the budgets of agencies like the Census Bureau and the BLS. Instead, once the budget is passed by the Congress and approved by the White House, the allocation of positions, together with other administrative issues, is left to be worked out with the Commissioner by the Secretary of Education and the Assistant Secretary for Educational Research and Improvement. As a result, NCES, from its inception, has had a very small staff and has found it difficult to carry out its legislated responsibilities.

The law provides that the Center ". . . acquire and diffuse among the people of the United States useful statistical information on subjects connected with education . . .", many of which are specifically mandated by statute (20 U.S. Code, chapter 31, par. (a)(1)). NCES is required especially to develop information on educational progress, financing of educational institutions, student aid, retention of students, supply and demand for teachers and other school personnel, and comparisons of education in the United States with education in other countries. NCES is also to develop information on ". . . the means of promoting material, social, and intellectual prosperity through education" (*ibid.*).

NCES has a statutory Advisory Committee made up of representatives of government agencies and of the educational community. In many cases, for example, the National Assessment of Educational Progress surveys, the Congress has also provided for special panels to provide guidance to NCES. The Center thus has advisors with more active agendas and more management-focus than do the other statistical agencies.[8]

The Center was reauthorized under the National Education Statistics Act of 1993, which the Administration sent to the Congress at the end of October 1993. The new bill essentially followed the earlier legislation. The National Center for Educational Statistics will continue to be situated within the Office of Educational Research and Improvement. and will continue to be headed by a presidentially appointed Commissioner who serves a four-year term. The Center has responsibility for collection, analysis, and dissemination of statistics related to education, including the condition and progress of education, state and local education reform, student achievement and other educational outcomes, student access to education, teaching, the learning environment, and the financing and management of education. The Center is specifically required to do longitudinal studies as well as other regular surveys and analyses. NCES works with the States to develop uniform standards and definitions and establishes cooperative data collection arrangements to survey schools for information on the nation's educational system. In addition, because of its small staff, the Center contracts with data collection and research groups in the private sector to carry out its responsibilities.

The new law also provides for strong confidentiality protection of data about individuals in the possession of the Center. Although the legislation contains a provision recognizing the right of the Secretary of Education, the Comptroller General of the United States, the Congressional Budget Office, and the Librarian of Congress to access the microdata in the hands of the National Center for Educational Statistics,[9] the restrictions against disclosure of information identifying individuals that apply to the Center are also applied by the law to NCES data in the hands of these outside groups. (Section (6)).

The task of the NCES, as the principal statistical agency in the field of education, has become increasingly important because of the tremendous interest in information on the state of education in this country. The demand for better statistical information on the quality of the U.S. educational system and for comparison of educational outcomes in this country with those in other countries has become a front-burner issue.

The National Agricultural Statistical Service and The Economic Research Service

Although statistical reporting of crop production was prescribed by Congress as early as 1862, NASS and ERS were not established within the Department of Agriculture until the early 1960s. Both have separate agency budgets. Each is headed by a career civil servant who reports to the Assistant Secretary for Economics, a policy officer appointed by the President with the consent of the Senate. Each agency has an extensive program, much of it prescribed by law.[10]

The NASS, with an FY 1995 appropriation of $81.4 million, has a mandate to collect and publish statistics in the general field of agriculture. NASS is responsible for surveys and censuses about production, supply and prices of crops and livestock, agricultural employment and wages, and other farm and growing conditions. The agency also does reimbursable work for other agencies requiring data on agricultural and farm conditions. For example, NASS has, from time to time, conducted surveys for the Department of Labor on a reimbursable basis on issues relating to the agricultural work force. NASS also works closely with the Census Bureau on the preparation for and handling of the agricultural census. The agency operates with a professional staff in Washington and through cooperative agreements with each of the states.

ERS, with an FY 1995 appropriation of $53.9 million, is a primary analytic user of NASS data and conducts its own surveys on farm issues. ERS does forecasts and analyses of demand and supply for farm produce, synthesizes and analyzes statistical information for agricultural policy and evaluation purposes, and produces statistical indicators on agricultural issues.

Economic research has been carried out in the Department of Agriculture since the early 1920s. Release of the crop forecasts has become famous because those forecasts were one of the first statistical products to affect stock market and futures contract prices. In order to prevent the possibility of premature release, the Agriculture Department, for a very long time now, has used a lock-up procedure. Those who come to the Department to review the forecasts are locked up until the exact time of release. Then they are free to report the news, and the Department can be assured that all users will have access to the information at the same time.[11]

The Energy Information Administration

The Energy Information Administration (EIA) is one of the newer agencies in the federal statistical system, having been created by law in 1977 as a part of the new Cabinet-level Energy Department. The Administrator of EIA is appointed by the President with consent of the Senate and, according to the law, ". . . shall be a person who, by reason of professional background and experience, is specially qualified to manage an energy information system."[12] The Administrator, who reports directly to the Secretary, does not have a fixed term of office.

With an FY 1995 appropriation of $84.7 million, EIA is by law responsible for managing a unified energy information program that collects and disseminates data on energy reserves, production, demand, and technology. The area in which it operates is important and frequently the subject of political argument. As a result, Congress put into the EIA legislation provisions designed to ensure the independence of the EIA Administrator in the collection of data and the publication of technical reports.[13] The law specifically provides that the Administrator has final responsibility for decisions about the choice of data to compile and does not need approval of any other department officer before releasing data to the public. This legislative provision is unique in the legislation applicable to the nation's statistical agencies.

EIA has had problems protecting identifiable data from other parts of the government, however. Soon after the agency was created, special arrangements were made to protect the confidentiality of data submitted to the agency from those in the Energy Department responsible for regulating the energy industry. But in 1990, the Justice Department insisted on access to energy price information from individual EIA reports for use against respondent companies. Although the Administrator of the Energy Information Administration, with the support of OMB's Statistical Policy Division and the heads of the other statistical agencies, tried to prevent that disclosure, the Department of Justice ruled that the Federal Administration Act of 1974 (P.L. 93-275) required the agency to turn the data over to the Justice Department. EIA was not able to convince the White House to intervene, although it was able later to work out arrangements with the Justice Department to provide non-specific company data. In August 1991, EIA informed all of its respondents to the surveys involved of the issue and of the Justice Department's interpretation of the law (Duncan 1993). These issues of confidentiality are extremely important to the viability of the entire statistical system. They will be discussed later in the book.

The National Center for Health Statistics

The National Center for Health Statistics (NCHS) is responsible for data in the broad field of health, on illness and disability and is the source for such vital statistics as births and deaths. Organizationally, NCHS is located in the Center for Disease Control within the Public Health Service of the Department of Health and Human Services. The NCHS Director, a career civil servant, reports to the Secretary through several levels of organizational structure.

Although NCHS is responsible for health and disability statistics as well as for vital records data, HHS relies for much of its data collection on units outside the statistical agency in other parts of the department. NCHS has also had a long-standing relationship with the Census Bureau, which collects the Health Interview Survey for NCHS. In addition, NCHS, like the National Center for Educational Statistics, contracts out a number of health surveys to the private sector.

The National Center for Health Statistics also has a federal-state cooperative program that enables it to work closely with the states to process many of the vital records needed for the health information database. Its responsibilities in this area have given NCHS particularly valuable experience in developing data from administrative records.

In recent years, many of the NCHS surveys have suffered budget cuts. In past years, some of the shortfall has been made up by the transfer of Public Health Service Evaluation Funds to NCHS. In FY 1995, for example, nearly $29 million of the agencies' funding came from the evaluation funds. This funding source can never be counted on, however, leaving NCHS in a somewhat precarious position.

As interest in data on health care has increased with the national debate on health care reform, data on health care issues have come increasingly into the public spotlight. Much of this work is being conducted outside of the National Center for Health Statistics, resulting in different definitions, different survey designs, and consequent comparability problems and confusion about such fundamental issues as the extent of health care coverage and medical outcomes for different groups of the population. The area of health care statistics is particularly dependent on large bodies of administrative data from government health programs like Medicare and Medicaid—highlighting the need to spend more time and resources on the issues surrounding integration of administrative and survey databases. The Department of Health and Human Services has given considerable attention to the development of new systems of data for health care monitoring—which raises important questions about availability of information, confidentiality protection, information required for regulatory action, and data on the condition of the health of the population. Since a good deal of this effort was linked to the Clinton Administration's proposals for health care reform, it is now unclear how the issues will be resolved.

ECONOMIC ANALYSIS, JUSTICE, AND INCOME

Bureau of Economic Analysis

The Bureau of Economic Analysis is in the Department of Commerce. Unlike the Census Bureau, however, the Director of BEA, by custom, has been a career civil servant appointed by the Commerce Secretary. The BEA Director reports to the Undersecretary of Commerce for Economic and Statistical Affairs.[14] The FY 1995 appropriation for BEA was $42.2 million, giving it one of the smallest budgets of the established agencies within the statistical system. In spite of its modest budget, BEA has the largest macroeconomic job in the entire statistical system. BEA is responsible for measuring the nation's income and product accounts, including its trade accounts. The agency is also the umbrella under which statistics produced by other agencies of the government are brought together into a system which essentially measures everything the economy does. Using the national income and accounts framework developed by Simon Kuznets a half century ago, BEA has become the keeper of the nation's economic accounts. Although BEA does some survey work, notably the survey of international investment, most of its work involves using data produced by other agencies in the federal statistical system and by program agencies of the government that produce statistics as a part of the administration of their programs.

As the nation's economic accountant, BEA must find measures to cover every activity in the country. Where data are not available, BEA is forced to make estimates from whatever data it can find. As a result of these very large responsibilities, BEA depends to a large extent on the information produced outside the agency for most of the information it requires—requiring it to work closely with other statistical agencies as well as with the regulatory and programmatic parts of the government which produce administrative data. As part of an economic statistics improvement initiative during the Bush Administration, a working group chaired by CEA Chairman Michael Boskin proposed, with support from the Bush Administration, that BEA funds be increased to permit improvement in the quality of the accounts, adoption of the UN System of National Accounts, enhanced balance of payments data, and expansion of the international investment and services data. But Congress (both the House and the Senate) reduced those budget requests substantially, and the BEA has not been able to realize all of the changes envisioned by the initiative.

The Bureau of Justice Statistics

For several years, the Law Enforcement Assistance Administration (LEAA) was the only agency dealing with statistics on the criminal justice system. Although it did analyze some statistical information, it had other responsibilities as well, and the statistical picture of the criminal justice system and its effect was, in consequence, very partial. As crime and punishment increasingly reached the spotlight of public concern, steps were taken to improve data compilation and analysis in this area. In 1979, the Bureau of Justice Statistics (BJS) was established "To encourage the collection and analysis of statistical information on crime, juvenile delinquency, and the operation of the criminal justice system." BJS—along with the Bureau of Justice Assistance (BJA), the National Institute of Justice (NIJ), and the Office of Juvenile Justice and Delinquency Prevention (OJJDP)—became part of the Office of Justice Programs within the Department. (42 U.S.C. 3722ff). The FY 1995 appropriation for BJS was $21.4 million. It expects to receive another $2.7 million from the Justice Department's salary and expense account, bringing its 1995 total to $24.1 million.

The Director of BJS is appointed by the President with consent of the Senate and, by law, is to report to the Attorney General through an Assistant Attorney General. In the enabling legislation, Congress made clear its intent to improve statistical information at all three levels of government—federal, state, and local—by providing authority for the establishment of national standards for the compilation and collection of data and by specific legislative provision for the Director to enter into agreements with other federal, state, local, and private agencies to collect and analyze data. Much of BJS's work is based upon administative records supplemented by BJS-sponsored special survey work. One of its most important surveys is the National Crime Victimization Survey collected by the Bureau of the Census through a reimbursable agreement with BJS. In addition to sponsoring programs to develop statistics using the databases developed elsewhere in the Department of Justice, BJS provides financial and technical assistance to support a national network of statistical centers in each state, which collects, analyzes, and disseminates information on criminal justice.

The position of BJS within the Department of Justice has been a matter of discussion within several Administrations and the Congress. In 1992, when the Administration bill to reauthorize the Office of Justice Programs was sent to Congress, the bill proposed removing BJS from OJP to give it "an independent status and organizational placement similar to that of other Federal statistical agencies, such as the Bureau of Labor Statistics, in the Department of Labor, and Bureau of the Census in the Department of Commerce." (Assistant Attorney General Rawls letter to the House and Senate, 1992.) The bill specifically provided for BJS to "be the principal national center for the collection, analysis, reposition, and dissemination" of statistics in the criminal justice field and for the Director of BJS to report directly to the Attorney General. (Section 301 and 302 of proposed bill). These provisions of the bill were not passed, and the status of the BJS within the Justice Department remains unchanged.

The Statistics of Income Division (SOI)

One of the oldest of the statistical programs in the United States, statistics have been compiled within the Treasury Department. Nearly a hundred years ago, when the first income tax legislation was passed in the United States, work began to classify and describe information on income. The Division itself, the outgrowth of the Bureau of Statistics created in Treasury in 1866, compiles and publishes statistical information based on tax returns and provides data to the Treasury Department and to the Congress on income, financial, and tax issues. The Division also analyzes such tax-related issues as foreign tax credit and sales of capital assets. Data are also developed for tax analysis purposes and for analysis of economic and financial issues in the household and business sectors of the economy. From the very beginning, U.S. income tax legislation provided for preparation of data on "the operation of the income tax law and containing classifications of taxpayers and of income, the amounts allowed as deductions and exemptions, and any other facts deemed pertinent and valuable . . ." (US statutes, vol. 39, part 1, ch. 463, Sec. 21, p. 776, 1917). The FY 1995 budget for SOI was $25.1 million. Although considered part of the federal statistical system until recently, SOI's functions are being merged with other parts of the IRS as part of a reorganization plan announced in 1993. As of FY 1994 the President's budget subsumed funds for IOS's statistical work into other IRS appropriations, and the Division is expected to change considerably.

The Statistics of Income Division specializes in the development and use of administrative statistics. Located in the Internal Revenue Service of the Treasury Department, the Division, headed by a career civil servant, has focused attention on statistical methods for using administrative databases, an area currently receiving increased attention as efforts continue to reduce respondent burden and to secure data for small areas of the country. SOI samples tax returns each year, reviews them for consistency, classifies them, and examines the data to protect individual privacy.

Bureau of Transportation Statistics

The newest statistical agency is the Bureau of Transportation Statistics (BTS), established by the Surface Transportation Efficiency Act of 1991. In establishing a broad mission for BTS—statistics and research on highway, rail, magnetic propulsion of transportation, and intermodal transportation systems—Congress emphasized the need for data that were free of bias, relevant to decision-making and acceptable to decision makers, timely, accurate, and comparable across different regions and modes of transportation. The Senate Committee Report tied the view that "past experience with government statistical bureaus suggest that certain organizational characteristics help to ensure that the data and statistical products produced by a Bureau will meet the desired objectives," to the fact that the Director of BTS was to be a person technically competent in the field, appointed by the President, "removable only for cause," and will report to the Secretary of Transportation (Report Transportation Act 1991, pp. 37–38). A very small agency still in its formative stage, BTS has an FY 1995 budget of about $15 million, appropriated by Congress from highway trust fund money.

AGENCY CHARACTERISTICS: SIMILARITIES AND DIFFERENCES

The agencies in the federal statistical system have developed along diverse paths. They differ from each other in size, scope, number of survey design experts and analysts, manner of appointment of the agency head, degree of independence, and status within each of the departments in which they are located.

Size of Appropriations

As shown back in table 3.1, the FY 1995 Congressional funding for statistics includes appropriated funds ranging from nearly $25 million to about $350 million (without counting the new Bureau of Transportation Statistics (BTS) in the Department of Transportation). The two agencies with the largest appropriations—BLS and Census—have budgets that are more than 10 times larger than the budgets of the two smallest agencies—BJS and SOI. Even the three next largest agencies (with FY 1994 funding of about $80 million each) have budgets only one-third the size of the two agencies with the largest budgets. It is also interesting to note that BEA, which confronts the monumental task of producing estimates for all economic activity in the country, must do so with only about one-sixth the appropriation size of Census or BLS.

Agency Head Appointment and Tenure

The directors of six out of the 11 statistical agencies are appointed by the President with the consent of the Senate. Of these six, only three—the Commissioner of the Bureau of Labor Statistics, the Commissioner of the National Center for Educational Statistics, and the Director of the Bureau of Transportation Statistics—have terms of office fixed by law at four years. The other three Directors—at Census, EIA, and BJS—are appointed by the President with Senate consent but serve at the pleasure of the President. As a result, these agencies get new leadership when the White House changes political hands.

The tenure of its head has important effects upon the agency and upon its statistical programs. Statistical programs take time to plan, to test, and to execute. Once the data have been collected, they need to be compiled, reviewed, analyzed, and made available to the public in both printed and electronic form. Those agencies directed by career civil servants tend to have considerable continuity of leadership. Among the agencies with presidentially appointed directors, as noted, only the Bureau of Labor Statistics has a long tradition of reappointment for its Commissioner.

The BLS experience, which includes reappointment without regard to party affiliation, is very different from that of the Census Bureau, where the Director changes with each new Administration and is selected at least in part by party affiliation. At the Department of Energy, the EIA Administrator changes after a new President has been elected, and the same arrangements hold at the Bureau of Justice Statistics.

It is still too soon to tell whether the pattern of reappointment will be followed when the four-year term of the Commissioner at the National Center for Educational Statistics expires in 1996 and the term of the Director of Transportation Statistics expires in 1998. The Congressional intent in establishing presidential appointments at these agencies was to build on BLS practice. It takes time to establish a tradition. However, the current Commissioner at NCES, the first to be appointed under the NCES law, who began his term only late in the summer of 1992, has announced that he will not seek reappointment when his current term expires.

METHODS FOR THE RELEASE OF STATISTICAL DATA

Critical to the operation of any statistical system is the manner in which the data it compiles is released. All users must have equal access to government data, and the agencies must ensure that no user can benefit financially or otherwise from access to material before the release time and date. Without such rules, it would not be possible to retain the objectivity and trust essential to a democratic statistical system. Just as important, however, is that the public trust the objectivity and the accuracy of the press releases issued by government statistical agencies. Public confidence is affected by many things—the statistical literacy of the user, the frequency of data revisions, the relevance of the underlying concepts, and the rules followed in the actual preparation and release of the data. In terms of organizational structure, however, the rules for preparation and release of government data play a significant role.

Major Economic Releases

The rules that govern the release of major economic statistical series in this country are unique among statistical agencies around the world. They serve the public well. Each year, agencies producing such series as the Gross Domestic Product, Employment and Unemployment, and Trade,[15] in consultation with the Statistical Policy Division of OMB, designate releases of data to be classified as principal economic indicators. Once so designated, the statistical release is subject to a series of procedural rules. Data are to be provided as rapidly after compilation as possible, and at least within 22 working days of the end of the reference period. The public is to be informed in advance of the release time and date. Each release is to include announcement of the timing of the next release in the series. Special procedures are used to prevent premature release of data estimates, including physical protection of the data until their release.

The most important elements of the process, clearly, are those involving the limitations on the government officials who receive information before the data are released to the public. By OMB order, the statistical agency provides information prior to release to the Chairman or to an official of the Council of Economic Advisors (CEA) designated by the Chairman, so that the CEA may inform the President. Until the data are provided to the press, however, the statistical agency is not permitted to provide the data to anyone else—not even to the head of its own department. In addition, to prevent political manipulation of the news, the order prohibits any political official from publicly commenting on the data until they have been in the public domain for at least one hour. Because of the increasingly large impact of these major economic releases on the world financial markets, all the major statistical agencies in the United States now provide the data to qualified reporters in a "lockup". For the Employment Situation release, for example, which has a public release time of 8:30 a.m., usually on the first Friday of each month, reporters may have access to the release at 8:00 a.m. but must remain within a specially provided locked area until 8:30.[16]

Major aspects of these release procedures were developed in response to some of the changes that had been made in the BLS release procedures during the Nixon Administration. The analysis in the BLS press releases had been criticized by White House staff, the BLS practice of presenting explanations of the data in press conferences had been eliminated, and changes had been made in BLS personnel concerned with employment and unemployment data. The professional community established a committee to examine the possible politicization of the release of data, and Congress held hearings on the subject. Although all agreed that BLS had not changed analysis or text, public concern over the objectivity of the release procedures was sufficient for many in the Ford Administration to feel that changes were needed. Under the leadership of Sidney Jones, then a CEA member, a solution was worked out which resulted in the OMB directive on release procedures for the major economic indicators. These release procedures are especially valuable during the periods of tension preceding important elections in which the data could affect political outcomes. And they have worked in spite of the fact that they rest not on law but rather on Executive Branch regulation.

Notes

1. Some of the bills in Congress would create a new Bureau of Environmental Statistics.

2. For the budget of an agency to be included in the list, net obligations for statistical activities in Fiscal Year 1990, 1991, or 1992 had to be at least $500,000 (OMB 1994).

3. As of the end of 1994, the Statistical Policy Division had a chief statistician and a personnel complement of 4 persons.

4. For example, the FY 1993 budget request for the current programs of the Census Bureau was $138.4 million; however, the Bureau of Labor Statistics requested more than $47 million for work to be performed for it by the Census Bureau, mostly for the labor force survey, consumer expenditure survey, and the point of purchase survey.

5. Although the 1990 Census enumerated a very large part of the population, the differential undercount for certain racial and ethnic groups was the subject of much public discussion and eventually ended up in the courts. The Director of the Census

Bureau recommended use of a statistical adjustment to adjust the numbers for the undercount but was overruled by the Secretary of Commerce and by the Undersecretary.

6. For a more complete discussion of confidentiality within the federal statistical system, see (Duncan 1993) and (JOS 1993).

7. The author served as Commissioner for more than 13 years under both Democratic and Republican Administrations. Her successor, the present Commissioner, was appointed by President Clinton.

8. The different roles played by Advisory Committees in the operation of different agencies of the federal statistical system are discussed later in this chapter.

9. Although the enabling legislation of the General Accounting Office provides for access to the data required to carry out the GAO mission, the fact that the Administration bill contains specific mention of the exceptions is important. The bill makes clear that the receiving agency is to provide the same degree of confidentiality as the original collection agency which made the confidentiality pledge.

10. Both the National Agricultural Statistical Service and the Economic Research Service were established to provide more effective coordination of research and statistics in the Department of Agriculture. The statistical service was then named the Statistical Reporting Service (see Secretary's memo 1961). SRS was renamed the National Agricultural Statistical Service in 1986.

11. As data have become more sensitive, and the effect on financial markets more direct, several other agencies, including the Census Bureau and the Bureau of Labor Statistics, have initiated lock-up procedures for the release of important indicators.

12. The Department of Energy Organization Act of 1977 incorporated into the Energy Information Administration the energy information and analysis which preceded EIA.

13. Paragraph 2 (d) of the 1977 Act states: "The Administrator shall not be required to obtain approval of any other officer or employee of the Department in connection with the collection or analysis of any information; nor shall the Administrator be required, prior to publication, to obtain the approval of any other officer or employee of the United States with respect to the substance of any statistical or forecasting reports which he has prepared in accordance with the law."

14. See, for example, Department of Commerce Organization order 1980.

15. The major economic indicators include some 10 to 20 indicators.

16. See Statistical Policy Directive 1985.

FEDERAL-STATE COOPERATION TO PRODUCE STATISTICS: CONFUSION OR SOLUTION?

Although the federal statistical system was established to collect data for the nation as a whole, it has been involved in data at the state and even local levels since the early part of this century. Two distinct factors lie behind this involvement.

The first is the U.S. system of government. Since there are clear limits on the federal role, policy responsibility—and the policy need for data that goes with it—is often at the state or local levels. This division of labor was embedded in the Constitution, and Congress has continued to reflect it in much of the legislation passed to deal with the nation's problems.

Second, and quite apart from this basic constitutional thrust, concerns about operational efficiency, respondent burdens, and expensive duplication of effort pushed federal statisticians to work out mutually advantageous relationships with the other levels of government, primarily the states. Different models of cooperation and coordination have been used by different agencies at the federal level, but the desire to maintain quality standards, as well as the need both to increase data coverage and to reduce respondent burden, required efficient *intergovernmental* procedures.

Federal agencies responsible for the nation's statistics recognized the need for coordination with state data collection agencies long before much thought had been given to the coordination of statistical work within the federal government itself. They found that the use of state organizations to collect information based on standards established by the federal government proved to be efficient in meeting the needs of both levels of government. The data produced by each state, when combined, formed a uniform system of data which was comparable across state boundaries. Today, as more and more of the policymakers in the federal government search for approaches to develop cooperation at the regional, state, and local levels for the delivery of government services, the success of the federal statistical system in dealing with intergovernmental units is instructive.

In recent years, federal programs have become increasingly dependent on state and local data. Today, for example, statistical data are used to allocate federal funds to states, and sometimes to counties and cities. They are used to determine eligibility for federal programs, to trigger programs on or off, depending typically on the level of economic activity, as well as to determine when local conditions require changes in federal public policies. And the concerns of the 1990s about the need for job growth and for assisting unemployed workers to find reemployment have again focused attention on reliable data relevant to local labor market conditions. Federal, state, and local governments all have a great deal at stake in the compilation of accurate and timely data at all three levels of government.

Although federal-state relationships in the area of statistical programs have developed in different ways for different agencies over the years, all agencies now recognize that cooperative programs only work well when cooperation is deliberately fostered and actually takes place. The "feds" frequently have a definite way of looking at things that can differ considerably from the state view of the same set of facts. History has demonstrated that cooperative statistical programs can flourish only when both federal and state perspectives have been taken into account. One serious problem, of course, has been the fact that federal and state needs for data do not always coincide. State and local data are generally quite expensive to collect because large samples need to be concentrated in small areas to provide reliable data at the local level. National data, in contrast, can be much cheaper to compile since fewer sample members are required in any particular area if the sample units can be spread throughout the country. Nevertheless, the federal statistical system has learned that successful federal-state cooperative programs must meet at least most of the needs of both partners. State officials have to explain local conditions to their constituencies and understand local economic and social conditions better than federal officials do. The federal partner, on the other hand, has more detailed knowledge of the needs of the national government and can help to ensure that the quality and uniformity of the data collected meet national standards.

Recent years of budget retrenchment, however, have strained the relationships that have taken so long to build up. Most federal government statistical surveys today are based on probability sampling. Because national data can be produced most easily and cheaply by spreading sample members across larger numbers of sampling areas, federal government agencies feel they have little choice but to reduce funding for local data while retaining data for the nation as a whole. In recent years, as Congress has legislated overall percentage cuts in department budgets rather than individual program budgets in order to meet legal budget restraints, budget retrenchment has hit data below the state level—for counties, metropolitan statistical areas, and neighborhoods—especially hard.

There is also a shared interest in using economies of scale to secure data that are consistent and comparable across different areas of the country. Given the decentralized nature of the federal statistical system, however, it should not be surprising to find that the models of federal-state statistical cooperation vary markedly from one agency to another. Each agency has a different arrangement for funding, the number of states involved varies by statistical program, the scope and coverage of the data collected differ, and different approaches are used to foster cooperation. Although some of the cooperative statistical programs have been in place for almost a century, many of the programs have different histories and different divisions of responsibility between the federal government and the state governments. Differences involve arrangements for joint management, standardized services, research, efficiency and stability, and building on the past (Coffey and Habermann 1990). But all levels of government recognize the imperative to reduce the duplication of effort and respondent burden that occurs when each level of government mounts its own surveys. And it is also well recognized that "the coordinating (federal) agency brings substantial resources to the negotiations as part of its contribution to the bargain" (Coffey and Habermann 1990, p. 11).

Almost all of the federal statistical agencies have some programs in which the states cooperate, but the form of the cooperation and the purpose and management of the programs differ from agency to agency. Some agencies work with the states to improve the comparability of data from administrative records, others cooperate in survey data collection, and still others have cooperative arrangements for the dissemination of statistical information. In the case of the National Center for Educational Statistics, for example, Congress has even created a legislative foundation for federal-state cooperative work.

Following are examples of three different types of cooperative programs.

LABOR MARKET STATISTICS—BUREAU OF LABOR STATISTICS

Beginning with cooperative arrangements with the state of New York in 1917, the Bureau of Labor Statistics (BLS) started cooperative work on its industry employment statistics program. As the role of the federal government in labor market issues expanded, the program was extended to all states and to other areas of labor statistics. After passage of the social legislation of the New Deal era—such as establishment of the Social Security system for retirement income and the Unemployment Compensation system for providing income to eligible unemployed workers during their period of job search—the program took on new emphasis and direction. The Wagner-Peyser Act provided federal funding for the Employment Security system in each state, and labor market information gradually became increasingly integrated with those programs.

In 1949, BLS successfully proposed use of some of the federal portion of the Unemployment Compensation trust fund to pay the states for work done on the federal-state cooperative Labor Market Information (LMI) program.[1] For many years, the funds were provided to the states through the Employment and Training Administration of the Department of Labor (the agency responsible for the UI system and for the job service), and the BLS provided technical supervision to the work of the states. As federal support funds came more and more under attack, however, Secretary of Labor Ray Donovon decided to transfer responsibility for Labor Market Information (LMI) funding from ETA to BLS, so that the financial and technical responsibilities for the programs could be managed efficiently within a single DOL agency. BLS staff worked with state staff to develop individual contracts with each of the states providing for program requirements, quality standards, and funding. BLS provides technical assistance and quality oversight through its regional offices, trains state personnel, and provides technical oversight to the program. Although each state must provide the data series agreed upon in the contract, it remains free to expand the programs to provide additional data at its own expense.

The system has worked well. The BLS has learned from the states about local labor market needs that require data, and the states have learned about new types of statistical estimation and sampling. In addition, BLS has been able to supply new technology to the states and to ensure increased accuracy and consistency through the use of standardized computer software. In many cases, BLS has contracted with individual states with advanced capabilities to design software for export to the other states and to undertake research projects to point the way toward program improvements. The quality of the cooperatively produced data has improved considerably in recent years, although much remains to be done.

AGRICULTURAL STATISTICS: NATIONAL AGRICULTURAL STATISTICAL SERVICE

The federal-state cooperative programs of the National Agricultural Statistical Service (NASS) began with the state of Wisconsin in 1917, the same year that BLS was beginning to cooperate with the state of New York. NASS worked with the states to provide more complete coverage of agricultural statistics, especially for its reports of crops and livestock. The core program is defined in a cooperative agreement between the two levels of government. Federal needs are specified and paid for federally, and individual states may pay the cost of producing more detailed information to meet its needs.

Unlike the BLS federal-state relationship, in which the federal government works out contractual arrangements for states to manage state activities and then provides technical support and oversight, the federal-state program in agricultural statistics is managed jointly by NASS at the federal level and by state employees at the state level. A federal statistician, a NASS employee, works on-site in each state to direct the program there, and other federal personnel are rotated among the states and between the state and federal offices. NASS handles research activities, survey design, survey implementation, and computer software. State employees also provide support for the joint programs.

VITAL STATISTICS ON HEALTH: NATIONAL CENTER FOR HEALTH STATISTICS

Because of the need for vital health statistics at all levels of government, the Cooperative Health Statistics System has been developed to provide the ground rules for cooperation in the collection of such statistics between the federal government and the states and localities. Dating from the turn of the century, the program began when several states requested help from the federal government in coordinating the many local systems of vital statistics. Since 1960, federal leadership for the program has been the responsibility of the National Center for Health Statistics (NCHS).

This system of sharing data among local, state, and federal units of government involves standardization of data collected through vital records systems as well as steps to improve their quality and their comparability among different areas of the country. In contrast to the labor market statistics programs, much of the cost of the vital statistics program continues to be borne by the states rather than by the federal government. One set of estimates indicates that states and local agencies pay up to two-thirds of the cost of the system (Coffey and Habermann 1990).

CONCLUSION

The three programs described above are similar and yet quite different. Each involves cooperative arrangements between the federal government and states and, in some cases, local governments. The cooperation involves determination of the scope of data to be collected, rules for consistency and comparability, and methods for improving the quality of the entire system. Management approaches range from management by federal employees (as in the case of NASS), state implementation of contractual arrangements with federal leadership in design and quality control (as in the case of the BLS), and state compilation of administrative records to further cooperative efforts (put forth by NCHS). Arrangements for funding of the programs also differ, with more federal funding available in the BLS and NASS programs than in the NCHS vital statistics program.

All three approaches are working well, demonstrating both the need for and the benefit of federal-state cooperation in the statistical arena. With the steadily increasing data requirements over the years, however, it is becoming clear that more cooperation in collection and compilation of data will be required to meet the demand for statistics at all levels of government—national, state, and local. Indeed, the current emphasis in the Congress to move more program development and management from the national government to the states makes it more critical than ever before that intergovernmental statistical cooperation be enhanced. Greater efforts at statistical cooperation will be required among the levels of government to develop comparable definitions and standards. Unless we have a more centralized approach to data development and preservation when programs are devolved to the states, the *country* risks the loss of substantial amounts of *national* data and the *states* will find it increasingly difficult to *compare* performance with other states. Federal legislation which moves national programs to the states must, therefore, recognize the need for comparable data across states, assign responsibility to the appropriate federal statistical agency, and provide the funds required for statistical information systems.

The existing federal-state cooperative programs must also adapt to this changing federal-state environment. We have learned that only the federal government can establish statistical standards for state and local governments to ensure that modern statistical techniques used at all levels of government produce data that are comparable across the country. And we also know that only the states and local areas know their own situations well enough to determine their needs. Our decentralized approach to intergovernmental statistical activities has yielded a variety of models from which lessons can be learned. The next step is to distill the best practices from the models we have and to use them to work toward an approach that promises further efficiencies and even higher statistical quality.

Note

1. A portion of the employer tax paid for the Unemployment Compensation system is reserved for federal distribution to states for administration of the system. In 1949, BLS proposed using some of these funds to help finance the compilation of labor market information statistics that would be comparable across all states.

Chapter Five

STATISTICAL POLICY COORDINATION: IS THE PRICE TOO HIGH?

The 10 federal agencies which have the production of statistics as their primary mission are joined by many times that number which produce statistics as a byproduct of regulatory or other program activities. In fiscal 1994, OMB listed 70 agencies spending more than half a million dollars each on statistical programs (OMB 1994). The task of pulling all the pieces of this widely dispersed system together into a cohesive whole falls to the statistical policy group[1] (SP) in the Office of Information and Regulatory Affairs at the Office of Management and Budget. This group has a very large mission and a very small staff to carry it out. At the beginning of 1995, SP had a Chief Statistician heading the office who was assisted by a staff of only four professionals.

This lack of resources hampers the statistical policy group's efforts to promote the quality and integrity of federal government statistics. It operates as best it can by asserting leadership and attempting to stimulate activity by individual agencies within the system. At times, when issues cut across the programs of several agencies, SP establishes a new committee made up of representatives from all the agencies with an interest in the issue and chaired by a staff member from one of the larger statistical agencies. Most recently, this approach has been used to prepare for revision of the Standard Industrial Classification system of all economic activity (SIC) and the Standard Occupational Classification system (SOC). The Chief Economist of the Bureau of Economic Analysis currently chairs the SIC Committee, and the Associate Commissioner for Employment and Unemployment Analysis of the Bureau of Labor Statistics heads the committee charged with revision of the SOC.

But the more difficult tasks of coordination, planning, and development of government-wide guidelines and standards for statistical work in the federal government—as well as evaluation of agency statistical output, budget review, and coordination of all legislative

proposals using statistics—must be done by statistical policy personnel themselves. Added to this agenda is the responsibility of the Chief
Statistician of OMB for coordinating statistical agency activities
abroad and for participation in a multitude of international statistical
meetings, in particular for representing the United States at the United
Nations Statistical Commission.

These are large responsibilities. The workload involved in coordination and planning for the 10 statistical agencies alone—to say nothing about the statistical work done elsewhere in the government—is
too large for the staff currently assigned to SP. Of necessity, therefore,
the statistical policy group has focused its attention only on program
issues of major importance. Insufficient time remains for work on
budget evaluation, survey innovation, data analysis, technological improvement, and information dissemination. This means that very few
resources in the statistical policy group can be devoted to the increasingly important issues raised by changing data requirements for public policy development and evaluation. It is indeed ironic that during
the years in which the public policy need for data grew more complex
and more important to government program implementation than ever
before, the OMB staff for these activities was steadily reduced.

How did this all come about? The history of official statistics in the
United States has clearly been affected by the country's opposition to
centralized power in the hands of the federal government. Agencies
were created where needed in those parts of the government dealing
with the particular issues involved. Except for the occasional studies
discussed in chapter 3, very little thought was given to coordination
of the system or to integration of the data it produced. Only when it
became clear that the New Deal programs required data for its programs to be carried out effectively was much thought given to coordinating the work of the government agencies producing statistics. A
Central Statistical Board (CSB) was established to review and coordinate statistics required for the National Industrial Recovery Act and
many of the other programs proposed by President Roosevelt. The
Board's functions were expanded to cover the entire statistical system
by executive order in 1934 and were transferred to the Bureau of the
Budget (now the Office of Management and Budget) in 1939. The
Federal Reports Act of 1942 further expanded the coordinating function and established the foundation for the operation of the office that
functioned to oversee the work of the federal statistical agencies.[2]

The work was not easy. In the early 1940s, the Director of the coordinating office referred to the federal statistical system as being ". . .
made up of a large number of semi-competitive, semi-monopolistic,

semi-integrated agencies, without very effective central control" (Rice, quoted in Duncan 1975). But as the government became more aware of these problems, the authority of the OMB division increased and the staff grew. By 1947, the staff approving survey forms, establishing classification structures, and coordinating federal statistical activities numbered 69.

The Federal Reports Act had given OMB power to plan, coordinate, and investigate both the statistical needs of the federal government and the methods for collecting and compiling the data required. Most important of all, the Act provided that no federal agency could undertake the collection of information from 10 or more respondents without approval of the Director of OMB. Thus, statistical agencies were forced to get OMB approval (through the Statistical Policy Division) before any significant new survey could be implemented. But the growth of the federal statistical system and the increasing complexity of statistical surveys made it difficult for the Statistical Policy Division to cope with its broad statutory responsibilities, even for the statistical agencies themselves, to say nothing of the program and administrative statistics programs that were spread increasingly throughout the nonstatistical agencies of the government.

A number of changes occurred after World War II, as the country's attention turned to peacetime issues and problems. Post-war conversion concerns and program needs required attention and funding. During this period, as wartime government activities were cut back, the budgets of some of the statistical agencies were drastically cut, and personnel was reduced. As time went on, however, the Office of Management and Budget (then called the Bureau of the Budget) added staff for its expanding coordination and oversight work. Gradually, the work of the statistical agencies increased and their personnel resources also expanded to produce new data series. The Statistical Policy Division's coordinating task became more difficult and much more important. But now, even as the responsibilities of SPD increased, the number of people on its staff began to decline.

Many of the increased coordinating responsibilities were established by law and presidential directives to implement the legislation. For example, Executive Order 10033 of February 6, 1949, as amended, required the Director of OMB to determine, with concurrence of the Secretary of State, how responses to requests for statistical information from other governments or from international organizations were to be filled and by which agencies. Section 103 of the Budget and Accounting Procedures Act of 1950[3] directs the President to develop programs and regulations to improve compilation, analysis, publication, and dissemination of statistics by executive agencies. Executive Order 10253, as amended, delegates the functions to the OMB Director to be redelegated to the Administrator of the Office of Information and Regulatory Affairs in which the Statistical Policy Branch now resides.

By the late 1970s, the resources for the statistical staff at OMB had been reduced by nearly 60 percent—from the 1947 high of 69 to 29 positions. And then, in 1977, when the President decided to reorganize the Office of Management and Budget, coordination of the statistical system was weakened still further. The statistical policy function reached a new low when the reorganization plan eliminated it entirely from OMB and transferred it to the Department of Commerce. There, it had no special authority over other parts of the system located in other departments and its staff was smaller than ever before. The forms clearance activity—that part of the statistical policy function which permitted the office to insist that the agencies follow its directions—was peeled off from the coordinating function and left at OMB. The staff was split between OMB and Commerce, with 14 members remaining in OMB to work on forms clearance as part of the paperwork reduction function and 15 members transferred to the Department of Commerce.

Although those at the Commerce Department responsible for statistical activity attempted to strengthen the effort by assigning additional positions to the coordination activity, it was very difficult to carry out the function from Commerce. Since that department also contained two statistical agencies—the Bureau of the Census and the Bureau of Economic Analysis—it was not able to present itself as a completely disinterested observer in providing leadership to the system.

Recognizing that things might have gone too far, the Carter Administration at this time decided that a thorough review of the organization and functioning of the government's statistical system was needed and asked James Bonnen to lead this multi-year effort, described more fully in chapter 3. The important point here is that the Bonnen group made a series of recommendations to strengthen the statistical system, the most important of which involved expanding the functions and importance of a new, enlarged, central statistical policy and coordinating agency to be located in the Executive Office of the President.

But the Bonnen recommendations were submitted to the Congress too late in the Carter administration for effective action, and the issue was left to the Reagan Administration. By this time (summer of 1991), Congress had passed the Paperwork Reduction Act, which required OMB to handle the statistical policy role as a part of its paperwork reduction responsibilities. The Paperwork Reduction Act requires the Director of OMB to carry out certain statistical policy and coordination functions. These include: 1) long-range planning to improve federal statistical programs; 2) review of statistical budgets; 3) overall coordination of all statistical functions of the federal government; 4) establishment of standards, classifications, and other guidelines for the operation and presentation of statistical data; 5) evaluation of statistical program performance; and 6) integration of these functions with other information management functions. In addition, the Act required the Director to appoint a trained and experienced Chief Statistician to carry out the requirements of the Act.

The Statistical Policy function is now carried out by a Chief Statistician who directs the Statistical Policy Branch within the Office of Information and Regulatory Affairs (OIRA).[4] Although the Reagan Administration established the policy branch within OIRA, it staffed the Branch with only 15 of the 26 positions that had handled statistical coordination issues at the Commerce Department. To make a difficult situation even worse, several of the remaining transferred positions were immediately reassigned to other work. And still more positions were eliminated during the remainder of the decade. Today, as noted, the Statistical Policy Branch operates with a professional staff of five.[5]

Almost every review of the structure of this coordination and of the structure of the statistical system has considered how well this decentralized approach to statistics serves the nation. Some have thought decentralization a strength, others a weakness. Some have focused on the difficulty in setting standards of quality and ensuring that they are enforced throughout the sprawling empire of statistics producers. Others have argued that the present organizational structure protects individual agencies against political influence. Still others have taken an exactly opposite position, arguing that centralization helped to ensure the absence of political influence on the release of data.

To examine this question, one must ask a number of questions about the functioning of the current structure and the data it produces. We need to know, for example, whether the current organizational structure gives adequate attention to public policy data needs and, if not, whether the solution is radical restructuring or merely changes around the edges. We need to know whether the system as now organized produces accurate and timely information relevant to the fast-changing social and economic environment of the country. Does the system provide data compiled by different agencies with incompatible con-

cepts and inconsistent classification structures, vastly complicating
the task of integrating data series into a cohesive whole? And we need
to know whether the decentralization of the statistical system leaves
agencies more or less open to political influence than would be true
of a centralized system. In short, does our statistical system work or
do we need to change it so that it can work?

Under the current organizational structure of our federal statistical
system, it is difficult for agencies to search for the most efficient and
least costly method of combining surveys and data sets across agencies. And given the lack of resources in the OMB authority responsible
for the coordination, there is no strong force equipped to study the
questions and to bring the agencies together to solve them.

Of course, the fact that inefficiencies of data collection exist or that,
at times, there appears to be a disconnect between data collected in
one agency and data collected in another does not, by itself, mean
that organizational change is needed. Indeed, the system has some
rather good examples of interagency cooperation, the recent redesign
of the nation's labor force survey being a case in point. Here, the
Bureau of the Census and the Bureau of Labor Statistics got together
to develop long-range goals, research plans, budget needs, and implementation of one of the most radical redesigns of an important official
survey ever undertaken by the federal government. The work was done
successfully benefitting from a long-standing background of experience of joint action by the two agencies (Norwood 1975, Norwood and
Tanur 1994).

But efforts of this sort, even when successful, are not sufficient to
prevent many of the inefficiencies which tend to characterize the statistical system. The few successes of cooperation and coordination
within the system do not provide convincing evidence that problems
do not exist.

This view is reinforced by the views of many of the senior officers
in the major statistical agencies. When surveyed by the author a few
years ago to ascertain their views about the federal statistical system,
many pointed to the need for a rationalization of the whole federal
statistical system and a rethinking of priorities. They pointed out that
policy issues seem more and more to be cutting across the traditional
lines and that integration of data was sometimes extremely difficult
to bring about. All agreed that steps needed to be taken to increase
the prestige and to improve the functioning of the federal statistical
system. Some favored strengthening coordination. Some felt that more
radical structural change in the system would be useful. And some
favored development of a new centralized federal statistical agency.
All pointed to the need to promote congressional understanding of

statistical agency operations and to their concerns about the erosion of statistical agency budgets. While the views of these senior officials differed depending on their own positions, agencies, and particular experience, all believed that strong action to strengthen the system is becoming more urgent every year.

Although almost every review of the U.S. federal statistical system has pointed to the need for better coordination of the nation's decentralized agencies,[6] the resources devoted to coordinating data produced across the system have not increased, and little improvement has occurred. Most of the studies discussed in chapter 3 have proposed strengthening and enlarging the coordinating group at the Office of Management and Budget. But, the size and power of the central coordinating group has risen and fallen with the country's changing interest in statistics. And in the last 25 years, even as the use of statistics in public policy has increased, resources for the coordinating function have steadily diminished.

The Statistical Policy Branch clearly recognizes the need for enhanced coordination within the system. But it has been unable to carry out the tasks required to pursue this objective, even though in recent years it has developed a cooperative relationship with the larger statistical agencies to use committees staffed by agency personnel to integrate classification and surveys within the system. But the research required to integrate data elements collected in different surveys, sometimes even using different definitions of the same phenomenon, is incredibly time consuming and difficult. It cannot be carried out by a small office with a director and a staff of four professionals.

Thus, the history of statistical policy coordination in the United States has been erratic, with periods of strength in the past but, in more recent times with periods of weakness. Action is urgent if the system is to continue its ability to carry out in the future the goal established a century ago by Carroll Wright, the first Commissioner of Labor Statistics, when he said: "To popularize statistics, to put them before the masses in a way which shall attract and yet not deceive, is a work every government which cares for its future stability should encourage" (Leiby 1960, p. 68).

Notes

1. Statistical Policy at the Office of Management and Budget has gone through several reorganizations over the years. The coordinating group now is named the Statistical Policy Branch in the Office of Information and Regulatory Affairs.

2. These functions were expanded and strengthened in 1942 and again in 1950; see Public Law 9312, December 24, 1942; Public Law 13, June 10, 1921; and Public Law 794, September 12, 1950.

3. 31 U.S.C. 1104 (d).

4. Section 3504 (d) of the Paperwork Reduction Act as amended; 44 U.S.C. 3504.

5. See articles by Katherine Wallman, James T. Bonnen, Stephen Fienberg, Courtenay Slater, and Christopher de Muth in *The American Statistician*, August 1993.

6. See Triplett (1991) for the view that the importance of coordination of the statistical system has been inflated and that the problems lie more in the way in which research on statistical issues is conducted and used as well as in the attitudes of individual statistical agencies.

Chapter Six

U.S. STATISTICAL INFRASTRUCTURE: HOW UNIQUE IS UNIQUE?

Statistical systems, like other parts of governments, are shaped by public attitudes about the role of government in social and economic problems, trust in government officials' ability to deal with public policy issues, and concerns about centralization and power. As a result, statistical systems around the world come in many shapes and sizes. Indeed, there seems no optimal formulation; too much depends upon the particular experience of the country and the attitudes of its people toward their government.

Even so, most large countries of the world have centralized their statistical activities into a single agency with broad authority for the collection and compilation of statistical data. Because one agency has the full responsibility for official statistics, coordination occurs within the agency itself, and economies of scale can be easily implemented. However, a few countries, the United States being a prime example, have a decentralized structure, in which statistical operations are dispersed among several government departments. In these cases, a coordinating group or agency exists with a mission to establish classification and quality standards, to monitor the respondent burden from government-sponsored surveys, and to oversee integration of a combined statistical budget that produces the data needed for public policy formulation. Countries with centralized statistical agencies place a great deal of coordinating power in their statistical agencies, but those with decentralized systems focus most responsibility in the individual departments of government. Sometimes in these decentralized systems, the coordination group manages a statistical personnel service across the agencies of government and, in this way, has a direct means of affecting the quality of the country's statistical output. But this is not the case in the United States. The statistical policy coordinating group in the United States is very small and has no control over those who work in the nation's widely dispersed statistical system. This country has one of the most decentralized statistical systems in the world and has also put the least resources into its coordinating arm.

The strengths and weaknesses of the different organizational systems for statistics have long been the subject of international debate. The *Economist* reported in the summer of 1993 that prominent international statisticians rated Canada first among 13 industrialized countries, and the United States only in sixth place, in a tie with Britain and Germany (*Economist* 1993, p. 65). Concerns about the U.S. statistical system, and especially allegations about inadequate coverage of statistics in the service-producing sector, continue to appear in the American press (e.g., *Business Week*, November 7, 1994). The reduced status of the statistical policy coordinating authority within the OMB organizational structure has contributed to the problems faced by the system both in coping with changing current economic and social issues and in defending the system against such criticism. Many years ago, the American statistical system would almost certainly have led the international community because of its innovative statistical research and its development of new approaches to sampling and survey design. In the last 25 years, however, other countries have focused considerably more attention and resources than the United States has on improving the quality and efficiency of their systems. The United States is still ahead in a number of areas, but its overall supremacy has certainly been lost.

In reviewing the problems of the U.S. statistical system and considering how to make it function more efficiently and effectively, it is important to compare our system's organizational structure with those in other countries. The most useful comparisons are those with Canada and with the United Kingdom. Both are industrialized democracies with economies that, while smaller than our own, are well developed. Canada has a centralized statistical system, and Britain has a decentralized one. Those who believe that centralization is the answer to American statistical problems cite the success of Statistics Canada as their example. Those favoring retention of decentralization cite the British system. In comparing the systems of both countries to our own, the differences in their size and in the scope and breadth of the statistics that must be produced should be kept in mind. Statistics Canada, for example, provides statistics for an economy that is only about one-tenth the size of our own and for a much smaller population. The Bureau of the Census alone, to say nothing of the other U.S. statistical agencies, is larger in size and in budget resources than the entire centralized Canadian statistical system. The British economy is about one-seventh as large as ours, and its population only about one quarter the size of ours. This reduces considerably the problems of developing and using data.

THE CENTRALIZED MODEL:
THE CANADIAN STATISTICAL SYSTEM

Although a national census for the Dominion of Canada was collected as early as 1870, and other statistical information had been collected as well, the modern statistical era in Canada really began with the Census and Statistics Act of 1905, which created a permanent office for censuses and other statistical information (Statistics Canada 1993). In 1912, the Foster Commission, pointing out that ". . . the statistics of a country . . . should constitute a single harmonious system . . ." recommended establishment of a central statistical office to be responsible for the statistical work of the government (Statistics Canada 1993). The first Chief Statistician of Canada, Robert H. Coats, oversaw the development of the new centralized system and remained at its helm until his retirement in 1942. Coats saw the benefits of centralization and moved to coordinate and expand Canada's statistical programs (Ryten 1990).

Today, Statistics Canada collects, compiles, and disseminates most of the official statistics of Canada. Although in a few cases, statistical data remain the responsibility of individual ministries, Statistics Canada has the power and scope of a prestigious central agency with vast responsibility for the nation's statistical system.

Statistics Canada, the agency responsible for providing and coordinating all official statistics in the country, works with other government ministries and with the provinces to produce the data needed for public policy. The Statistics Act was revised in 1971 to provide for federal-provincial statistical cooperation and to modernize confidentiality procedures. As the central statistical agency of Canada, Statistics Canada has access to government administrative data including tax returns and, with careful procedures to prevent disclosure of individual records, can use them in the development of statistical series. The scope of the agency is very broad. Unlike the situation in the United States, the National Accounts, the Census of Population, labor force surveys, and agricultural statistics—to mention just a few of its programs—are all compiled in this single statistical agency.

The Agency is headed by a Chief Statistician who reports directly to the Minister designated to carry out the responsibilities set forth by the Canadian Statistics Act.[1] The Chief Statistician supervises the staff of Statistics Canada, advises the government on the statistical programs of the departments and agencies, confers with them, and provides leadership in the development of national and provincial data. The Chief Statistician position does not change when the government changes. Indeed, the Chief Statistician position has considerable longevity; Canada has had only nine Chief Statisticians over the last 70 years.

Statistics Canada, as a large agency with broad statistical responsibilities, has the ability to examine funding priorities across almost all of the Canadian statistical system. Moreover, a centralized system can benefit from economies of scale that are difficult to achieve in a decentralized system. In recent years, as a part of its efforts at budget retrenchment, the Canadian government has required recovery of a significant portion of survey costs from user fees—a controversial issue in democratic societies.[2] One knowledgeable estimate is that about 8 percent of the total budget of Statistics Canada comes from user fees (Ryten 1990).

Many reasons have been put forward for the centralization of statistical activities. Comparison of the U.S. system with that of Canada usually focuses on the more efficient approach to budget priorities, the benefits of large-scale systems, and the ability of a central agency to make arrangements with regulatory and other governmental bodies for the effective use of administrative data. In considering the organizational structure, a senior official of Statistics Canada has said:

> Were Statistics Canada to be fragmented, and its various components attached to different departments, it is very likely that at least in the short term some or even many of those departments would be better served in terms of the relevance and timeliness of the information provided to them. It is less likely that in the long term, such departments could sustain the infra-structure and necessary degree of professionalism to keep statistical satellites in working order. But it is equally likely that given its stance and network of contacts, Statistics Canada as it is currently organized is in a better position to meet the requirements of its many constituencies." (Ryten 1990, p. 326)

The legislative foundation under which Statistics Canada operates is important to understanding its effectiveness. In the United States, each operation has different enabling legislation, different legislative authority, and generally is housed in a different executive agency. Clearly, our system could benefit by adopting some of the Canadian techniques of operation. But it would be a mistake to believe that we could simply import from Canada intact a structure and legislative foundation that appears to work well there. The two countries differ in size and governmental structure as well as in the legislative foundation and traditions of their statistical systems. The U.S. system could benefit from the Canadian experience, but these deep differences would have to be taken into account in any redesign of the American system.

The centralization-decentralization issue is sometimes presented as a means of solving all problems of efficiency, relevance, and trust in data. This is a misleading oversimplification. While it is clear that decentralization causes weaknesses, it also produces strengths. The most important benefit of decentralization is, of course, the speed with which data requirements for policy determination can be considered and, in fact, delivered. But familiarity with statistical techniques, and the objectivity with which they are likely to be applied can be developed more easily in a central statistical agency.

In considering alternative models for the organization of a national statistical system, one must always remember that organizational structure, by itself, cannot always solve all the problems a system faces. Indeed, it was not too many years ago that Statistics Canada fell on hard times. The Canadian people's concern about the system became so prevalent that the Government of Canada asked a group of three prominent non-Canadian statisticians/economists to review the system and to make recommendations for improvement.[3] While pointing to Statistics Canada as "one of the leading statistical agencies in the world" the group, chaired by the former head of the British statistical system, Sir Claus Moser, found several management and morale problems at Statistics Canada (Statistics Canada 1993). A new Chief Statistician, Martin B. Wilk, was appointed, and he embarked on a vigorous program of improvement to ensure public trust. Under Wilk's leadership, and with much hard work, the reputation of Statistics Canada was restored. The incident demonstrated clearly, however, that problems can arise in any statistical system regardless of its organizational structure. It is the people who make a system, and the structure can only help or hinder operation of the agency.

A DECENTRALIZED MODEL: THE UNITED KINGDOM'S STATISTICAL SYSTEM

The statistical system in the United Kingdom is very different from that of Canada. In the United Kingdom, statistical operations—data collection, processing, analysis, and publication—can be found in many places in the government. Statistics are located in perhaps 30 ministries and departments. Thus, the UK, like the United States, has a decentralized system with a large number of units acting independently of each other.

But there are important differences between the two systems. The U.K. has a strong central coordinating arm, the Central Statistical Office (CSO), and, in the tradition of the British Civil Service, has a unified Statistical Civil Service which is administered by the CSO. The CSO protects the Civil Service from undue politicization and has authority to move those in the Statistical Service from one position to another as the requirements of the entire system change. No similar personnel authority exists in the United States. Unlike the Statistical Policy Branch in the U. S. Office of Management and Budget with its very small staff and no survey collection responsibilities, the CSO has a sizable staff, authority over all statistical personnel wherever located, and power to carry out major statistical compilation and collection in its own right.

The fact that organizational structure does not by itself prevent dissatisfaction and criticism of a statistical system can be seen in the recent difficulties experienced by the United Kingdom's official statisticians. A series of changes to the nation's unemployment statistics and the creation of a tax and prices index, together with radical cuts in statistical operations, raised questions about the integrity and quality of official statistics. Many objected, as well, to the conclusion of Sir Derek Raynor in his December 1980 report to the Government that "Information should not be collected primarily for publication. It should be collected primarily because government needs it for its own business" (Raynor Report 1981, p. 15). After considerable discussion in the press and the statistics profession, a series of changes were made to reestablish public confidence in the system. In 1989, the Central Statistical Office was given direct responsibility for most of the macroeconomic statistics (the national accounts) and associated business statistics.[4]

A further change was made in 1991, when the Central Statistical Office was established as a separate department reporting to the Chancellor of the Exchequer. The CSO Director now manages an executive agency in addition to having responsibilities as head of the Government Statistical System, being the country's chief statistical advisor, and serving as "head of profession for government statisticians" (RSS Journal 1991, pp. 181–184).

Although both the United States and the United Kingdom have decentralized statistical systems, the contrast between the two countries is stark. The CSO has little authority over the various statistical activities located in other ministries, but the Director of the Office serves as an important officer of the government, has a fixed term of office, and has the right of access to the Prime Minister himself on issues involving the quality and integrity of the nation's statistics. Indeed, the custom in the United Kingdom is to bestow knighthood upon the person who heads the CSO.

* * *

It is clear that the United States is closer to the decentralized model of the United Kingdom than it is to the centralized organization of Canada. But the American system is far more decentralized than that of the United Kingdom, and its Statistical Policy Branch is far weaker than theirs. The Chief Statistician of Canada has a position of considerable prestige within his government, and the centralized agency has far more power even than that of the United Kingdom. Although not so powerful as the Chief Statistician of Canada, the Director of the CSO in the United Kingdom has more stature than the U.S. Director of SP. He reports directly to a Minister of Government, whereas the Chief Statistician at the Office of Management and Budget reports to an Office Director. Furthermore, the CSO Director's control over personnel in the U.K. statistical service strengthens his hand considerably. Indeed, the fact that the United Kingdom has a separate, professional statistical civil service, and that the CSO Director heads it, is an important aid in his ability to coordinate the system effectively.

The weakness of the American system is quite clear when compared to either of these other countries. Nevertheless, it is important to stress again that the different organizational structures of Canada and the United Kingdom have not been sufficient to insulate official statisticians in either of those countries from criticisms of the quality, the integrity, and the objectivity of their output. Organizational structure can do much to enhance the quality of an official statistics system either through centralization in a single agency or through strong and effective coordination in a decentralized system. In either case, statistical agencies cannot operate from ivory towers and expect the data they produce to be relevant to current policy. They must analyze as well as collect and compile data, for it is only from such activity that emerging trends can be identified and the statistical series kept relevant to current issues. These analyses are more likely to be undertaken and evaluated against current developments in a decentralized system. But a strong structure for managing data development and compilation, which can do much to enhance the quality of an official statistics system, is easier to achieve in a centralized environment. Along with an efficient organizational structure, an effective statistical system needs also to cultivate a culture of professionalism and a staff dedicated to the production of accurate and relevant statistics in an open and objective manner. Political pressure is likely to be applied less often, and more attention is likely to be paid to statistical and survey research in a centralized than in a decentralized system. It may also be easier to build up and maintain public support for data when the focus is on one agency rather than on a conglomerate of them. Under these circumstances, it is likely that such a culture can be more easily developed and maintained in a centralized statistical system than in a system with many separate organizations.

Notes

1. Statistics Act 1985, c S-19 amended 1988, c 65, s 146; 1990, c 45, s 54; 1992, c 1, ss 130, 131.

2. The use of user fees has received considerable public discussion in the United States as efforts toward budget retrenchment have picked up. See, for example, OMB Circular A-130, Revision of July 2, 1993, which states in Section 7, par (b) that the "free flow of information between the government and the public is essential to a democratic society." U.S. policy on user fees is stated clearly in Section 7 , par 8 (7) (c): user charges should be set to "recover the cost of dissemination but no higher. They shall exclude from calculation of the charges costs associated with original collection and processing of information" (Federal Register, volume 58, No. 128, Friday, July 2, 1993). The issue was considered carefully by an interagency committee of the federal statistical system chaired by William Barron, Jr., Deputy Commissioner of the Bureau of Labor Statistics.

3. Sir Claus Moser, retired head of the British statistical system, Dr. Joel Popkin, President of an American economic consulting firm, and Dr. Margaret Martin, recently retired from a long career in statistical policy at the OMB, were the group consulted.

4. See discussion of public confidence in the statistical system in *Journal of the Royal Statistical Society* 1990, volume 153.

Chapter Seven

ORGANIZING TO COUNT: HOW CAN WE IMPROVE THE FEDERAL STATISTICAL SYSTEM?

Until about 40 or 50 years ago, the federal statistical system worked reasonably well. The population census required by the Constitution was compiled once each decade, and specialized government statistical agencies compiled a number of useful statistical series—for example, on food prices and farm products. The federal government did not play an activist role in social and economic policy, and few issues of national interest required statistics for analysis or program implementation. The statistical information system, although decentralized and at times inefficient, was able to handle the need for statistical information (Norwood 1990).

The system worked well for many reasons. Statistics as a science only began to develop in this country in the latter half of the nineteenth century, and the demand for data at that time was not very large. Americans were not accustomed to using statistics to understand the economy or to learn about the conditions in which they lived. Following the great depression of the 1930s, however, the federal government became more involved in economic and social policy, and the need for data escalated. The government required data for program implementation, the private sector's demand for information increased, and the American people began to recognize that information reflected in the country's statistical series could result in new programs or program changes that would affect their everyday lives and livelihoods.

As a result, the public spotlight focused increasingly on the inherent problems of coordinating activity and setting priorities among statistical programs spread throughout the executive branch. More recently, the business community has joined the critics of government-produced statistics and of the rising burden of reporting information for government surveys. Associations, representing professional users of data, have become concerned about priority setting among statistical programs and about the problems of accessing and integrating various data sets. Even those working within the statistical system have become more outspoken about their frustrations in adapting to a new technologically driven world, and to the problems of dealing effectively in an increasingly internationalized environment.

Against this background, one might ask why so little has been done to change the way the system operates. Many reasons underlie this inaction. The United States' economy is very large and its population is diverse. The country does have a broad array of statistical information and, in general, statistical agencies do many things very well. People are, after all, creatures of habit, who are always most comfortable with things that are known. The country has become accustomed to a system with years of experience of working in old ways. Each statistical agency has a different organizational structure, its own style of operation, and functions differently from the other statistical agencies within its own parent department. Realignment of survey design, data compilation, and publication arrangements could be difficult and, in the short run, even expensive. This suggests that change in the system will be most successful when it reflects insights learned from experience and when implementation is gradual.

Some argue that the U.S. statistical system needs radical change, and that it should be completely centralized. There are good reasons to favor centralization. The more a system is centralized, the more efficient it can be in integrating its research, methodology, and survey designs and in taking advantage of economies of scale. Statistical systems with a high degree of centralization are better positioned to avoid duplication of effort and to undertake statistical and technological research. But there are advantages of decentralization also. A system that is decentralized, in which the data collection function is in the same department or agency as the policy responsibility, can relate data more easily to policy issues than one that is centralized in an agency separate from the department with policy responsibility. For this to work well, however, a decentralized system must rely heavily on the authority, status, and effectiveness of the coordinating authority.

The U.S. system has neither the advantages that come from centralization nor the efficiency that comes from strong coordination in decentralization. As presently organized, therefore, the country's statistical system will be hard pressed to meet the demands of a technologically advanced, increasingly internationalized world in which the demand for objective data of high quality is steadily rising.

Change is needed. But in determining the kind of change and the manner in which that change should take place, the focus must be on the central problem. The current structure of the federal statistical system is inefficient and ineffective. There are only two options. Either a start should be made toward moving to a centralized system or an effective method must be developed to strengthen the coordination of the existing system.

The first approach—a move to centralization—is both revolutionary and swift. It involves radical surgery to the organizational structure by carving out of several existing departments a new "Statistics America." Under this approach, several of the major statistical agencies would be moved from their departments and combined to form an independent Central Statistical Board (CSB). This board would produce directly most of our most important and broadest-based statistical programs and, in addition, would have the authority—and the resources—to coordinate, prioritize, and oversee the quality of the statistical work of specialized agencies outside the CSB. This approach would constitute the most effective solution to the problems of the federal statistical system. It fits in comfortably with the current efforts of officials from both the executive and legislative branches of our government to reshape government to promote efficiency and accountability.

Opposition to such a solution is likely from at least two quarters, however. First, creation of a new statistical agency, no matter how desirable, could raise concerns among those who want to reduce the number and size of government agencies. The host departments of the statistical agencies that would be moved into the new departments can also be expected to oppose this solution. They will argue that it will be difficult—perhaps impossible—to maintain the relevance of data to policy issues in a centralized environment. If such opposition develops, a less traumatic approach could also prove effective. Under this alternative scenario, each of the existing agencies would remain in its current parent department, and special legislation would be passed to standarize procedures, strengthen coordination, provide uniform confidentiality protection across the system and provide rules for the appointment of statistical agency heads and for the operation of the agencies. Both approaches would require congressional action. And even under the revised structure of the Congress put in place early in 1995, this action would involve at least six or seven congressional committees.[1]

STRENGTHENING THE STATISTICAL SYSTEM THROUGH ORGANIZATIONAL CHANGE

This section presents a proposal to strengthen the statistical system through centralization. The proposal envisions a modified Statistics

Canada approach—a Statistics America that would house the large general-purpose statistical series, the national accounts, and the federal government's statistical coordinating arm in a single super-agency, the Central Statistical Board (CSB). Although there are arguments in favor of much more complete consolidation, I do not pursue such a proposal here. The reason is that, even with a Congress ready to adopt new approaches to government, the size of the resulting government agency would be enormous enough to present formidable management problems. In addition, the political problems involved in taking important bureaus and agencies from a large number of Cabinet agencies seem insurmountable. The most that can be expected would be evolving consolidation over time, with the CSB I describe in this section serving as the impetus and the magnet.

The new CSB, as I envision it, would have broad authority to collect, compile, analyze, and disseminate statistical information. Its core—and the core of the federal statistical system—would be the Bureau of the Census and the Bureau of Labor Statistics. The Census Bureau now produces large bodies of data on production, sales, trade, etc. and serves as the specialized center within the government for household survey work sponsored by the United States government. These programs would continue as a part of the work of the Central Statistical Board. The Bureau of Labor Statistics programs cover such important areas of the economy as employment, inflation, and productivity. They would also continue as a part of the CSB work, as would the specific BLS surveys and analyses on such subjects as wages and fringe benefits. Both agencies have the capacity to design surveys, to collect data through a cadre of interviewers working out of regional offices throughout the country, to process the data collected, and to analyze and disseminate the information.

The placement of both these agencies in a new Central Statistical Board would make it possible to develop and carry out a comprehensive, systematic effort to combine surveys and develop economies of scale. Such a CSB would be in a position to undertake the careful evaluation and research needed to make decisions about more efficient survey design and about ways to eliminate duplication and reduce the data collection burden on survey respondents. Such a process is extremely important, because the data these agencies produce are among the most sensitive and the most critical of all data produced by the U.S. government.

In addition to these two large agencies, the CSB would also include two smaller groups which, though smaller, have very broad responsibilities. The Bureau of Economic Analysis, which compiles the national accounts, must work with all the agencies in the system because of its need to estimate the national income and product accounts. BEA products have tremendous national policy impact. BEA must be an integral part of the CSB to enable it effectively to influence priorities for the broad array of statistical information required for the national accounts.

An additional member of the CSB would be the Statistical Policy Branch currently located in OMB. The SPB has important responsibilities for oversight of the objectivity, quality, and utility of all the statistical work of the United States government and would, in cooperation with the other members of the Board, help to determine priorities for data across the system. Operating from the CSB, and clothed with the authority vested in the CSB by its enabling legislation, the new Statistical Policy Directorate would be a far stronger coordinating force than is now the case. It would also continue its responsibilities for creating classification structures and for overseeing the quality and statistical methodology for all statistical work done by the U.S. government, both inside and outside the Central Statistical Board.

This CSB would be large in size and budget. The combination of the two largest bureaus in the system, for example—BLS and Census—would result in a CSB budget of more than $1.0 billion a year for regular ongoing activities (see figure 7.1). This budget would be augmented considerably during the decennial population census years. Together these agencies directly employ some 10,000 people and pay for thousands more on the payrolls of individual states working on cooperative statistical programs with the federal government. The budgets and staff of the Bureau of Economic Analysis and the Statistical Policy Branch are small. They would add about $50 million and between 50 and 100 employees to the Central Statistical Board.

Each of the agencies in the CSB under this plan would be headed by a Director (or a Commissioner) who, in addition, would serve as a member of the Board of Directors of the Central Statistical Board. The Bureau of the Census would be divided into two Directorates—one for research and preparation for the collection and analysis of the decennial population census and the other for managing the ongoing work of the Census Bureau. This management work includes the business and agriculture censuses and surveys carried out by the Census Bureau's economic group, as well as the household survey work done for the Census Bureau and for other agencies within the system. Gradually, as cooperative experience at working together within the CSB develops, subject-matter staffs within the Census Bureau and the Bu-

Figure 7.1. Central Statistical Board

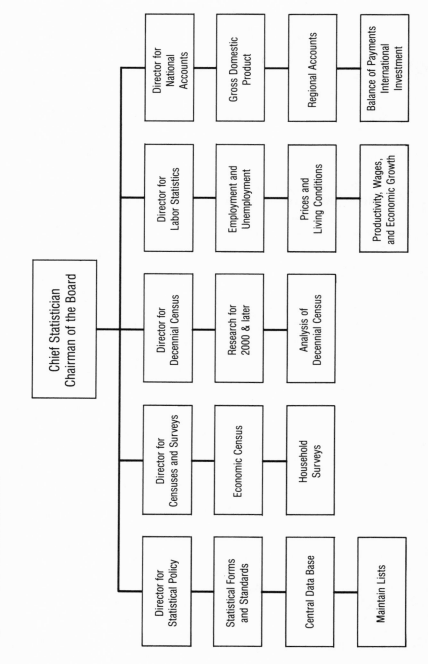

reau of Labor Statistics could be combined for various topics, first on a temporary basis and then more permanently.

The CSB itself would be headed by a Chief Statistician, who would serve as Chairman of the Board and be chief spokesman for the federal statistical system both at home and abroad. All Directors would be appointed by the President with consent of the Senate and would serve for a fixed term of office of at least 5 years and perhaps of 10 years. The President would also name with Senatorial consent the Chief Statistician and Chair of the Board of Directors.

Functioning as an independent Board or Commission, the CSB would handle all of the data systems currently produced by the Bureaus of the Census and of Labor Statistics and all elements of the national accounts currently produced by the Bureau of Economic Analysis, including international balance of payments estimates and data on international investments. The CSB would also coordinate and prioritize the large amount of statistical work done by the 7 other agencies in the statistical system and by programmatic agencies outside the CSB. Thus, the Board of Directors of the CSB would evaluate and recommend to the President and the Congress budget priorities for the nation's data systems and oversee the maintenance of the quality and objectivity of the data produced by the U.S. Government. All contacts with foreign statistical agencies would be handled by the CSB, sometimes with the assistance of other statistical agencies or other parts of the U.S. government. The CSB would be the depository for an integrated statistical information system, oversee the agencies in carrying out the pledges of confidentiality made to respondents providing data to the government, and would carry out the other functions handled currently by the Chief Statistician at the Office of Management and Budget.

Two other elements of CSB power are critically important. The OMB authority for statistical survey forms clearance must be lodged in the CSB, and the legislation establishing the CSB must replace the piecemeal confidentiality protection laws currently in place among the different statistical agencies. The new provisions would permit the exchange of confidential information, under carefully controlled procedures to be approved and administered by the Board, for statistical purposes only. In addition, the enabling act for the CSB would provide the fire-wall protection that is needed to protect the use of data collected strictly for statistical purposes from being used in enforcement actions against survey respondents.

Centralization of the core statistical agencies into a new Central Statistical Board to produce a significant number of the important elements of the government's statistical database directly, and to co-ordinate other statistical operations, could solve many of the issues I have raised in this book. The enabling legislation would have to be very comprehensive, providing the new board with effective authority to carry out its responsibilities for its own work and for statistical work carried out elsewhere in the government. Such a plan would go a long way toward providing an organizational framework for solving many of the problems that have long plagued the federal statistical system.

AN ALTERNATIVE APPROACH IF NEEDED: PASSAGE OF A NEW NATIONAL STATISTICAL LAW

If the preferred solution proved too traumatic for the Congress and the Executive Branch bureaucracy to accept, a less drastic alternative could prove effective. Each agency could remain in its current parent department. But a National Statistical Improvement Act would be passed. The provisions of this act would be designed to provide for uniform confidentiality protection across the system and for the ex-change of microdata within the system for statistical uses, standardize the manner in which statistical agencies operate within their respec-tive departments, strengthen the role of the chief statistician at the Office of Management and Budget, and protect the objectivity of major statistical releases. This National Statistical Improvement Act would bring the United States into closer conformity with legal provisions in other countries, where statistical systems are generally based upon a national statistical law.

Because of the complexities of the legislative process—as well as of the significant number of executive branch stakeholders who might wish to retain control over the statistical bureaus now in their own departments—it is possible that this less radical solution—based on legislative authority rather than organizational change—could be im-plemented very quickly. It could go far toward eliminating barriers which impede the efficient and orderly functioning of the statistical system. It could even be considered a first step toward a more cen-tralized organizational structure.

Standardization of Confidentiality Protection and Exchange of Microdata

Protection of the confidentiality of the data collected for statistical purposes is basic to development of data of high quality in any statistical system. Unless respondents can be assured that the data they provide to the government for statistical purposes will not be used for regulation or enforcement, the information they report will not be accurate, and the statistical series produced will contain unnecessary bias. Such protection is not uniform or uniformly effective in the current system, because the agencies in the decentralized U.S. statistical system originated at different times with different legislative foundations. As a result, the system operates with a complex set of regulations, executive orders, and laws which differ among the agencies. At one extreme, as with Title 13 of the Census Bureau, legislation to protect respondent confidentiality has been interpreted to prohibit other agencies from access to survey microdata even for surveys they sponsor and fund and pay the Census Bureau to collect. At the other extreme are agencies, like the Energy Information Administration, where the protection is not strong enough to prevent the use of such data in enforcement proceedings against respondents. In between are agencies like the Bureau of Labor Statistics, which has a long history of successful reliance on executive order, custom, and case law for confidentiality protection. At times, as in the case of the National Center for Educational Statistics, where the law spells out clear confidentiality protection, Congress itself has stepped in to weaken confidentiality protection retroactively when stakeholder pressure becomes sufficiently great. Thus, some agencies (Census, NCHS) have very restrictive confidentiality laws, others (BLS) have successfully defended confidentiality without specific legislation, and still others (EIA) have found it difficult in the executive branch of government to separate data collected for statistical purposes from use in enforcement or (NCES) have found it impossible to ensure against adverse action on the agency pledge of confidentiality by the Congress.

Uniform protection applied in the same way to confidential data collected by each of the agencies in the system is essential. Respondents who supply data to the federal government for statistical purposes need legislative assurance that those data will not be released in identifiable form, and that the same protection applies to all federal statistical agencies. As government regulations have increased, many businesses have become concerned about the confidentiality of the data they supply to the government. In addition to assurances that the data will not be made available to their competitors, these respondents want legal protection against the use of the data provided for statistical purposes in government regulatory or legal action against them. The large companies now clear all government survey requests with their legal departments before agreeing to participate in the data collection. If respondents could familiarize themselves with a single, uniform system based upon a single law—no matter which of the statistical agencies made the confidentiality pledge—their need to seek legal review of the provisions for confidentiality protection would be significantly reduced.

Just as important as the confidentiality itself, differences in confidentiality laws and policies among the agencies hamper and, in some cases, absolutely prohibit the exchange of protected microdata among the statistical agencies. As a result, agencies must either forgo the use of data already collected in other parts of the system or, when that is not possible, re-collect the data needed because they cannot get them transferred from another agency. The burden on respondents is thereby increased, and many, deciding that the government statistical system is inefficient and incompetent, decide not to cooperate at all in government surveys unless required to do so by law. In addition, costs are escalated because of unnecessary re-collection of data. And agencies cannot undertake comparative microdata research, universe list comparisons, or work to ensure uniformity of classifications with data collected by two or more different statistical agencies.

This need not be the case. The federal agencies whose basic mission is the collection and dissemination of statistics should *and can* have legislatively based uniform confidentiality protection, which a) protects respondents from government release of data in a form that permits users to identify the respondents; b) creates a "firewall" between the statistical and regulatory use of data, making it illegal for anyone to use data collected for statistical purposes for regulation or enforcement; and c) permits the exchange of data **for statistical purposes** among the agencies of the system under carefully prescribed written procedures.

These issues of confidentiality and data sharing have a long history; they have been discussed many times within the statistical system. I myself have participated in efforts to consider and resolve these issues within the executive branch. Many of these efforts led to draft proposals for data exchange, but no bill was ever proposed to Congress for passage. Seemingly insurmountable bureaucratic problems—such as the authority of a Cabinet Secretary versus that of the Director of OMB, or the reluctance to amend Title 13—always prevented action.

Many in the system believed that objections to the exchange of data were finally brushed aside, when the proposal for carefully protected exchange of microdata within the statistical system was approved in the Council of Economic Advisors statistical initiative known as the Boskin plan. But, as often happens with statistical reform, the principle adopted came too late in President Bush's term for full preparation and active consideration of the required legislation. Since that time, statistical budgets have become much tighter, and some of the individuals most opposed to legislative action have left the statistical system or changed their positions on the issue. In addition, a study by the respected Committee on National Statistics has recommended action to permit the exchange of data for statistical purposes (Duncan 1993). The time is now truly ripe, therefore, to pass legislation ensuring uniform confidentiality protection for statistical agencies and permitting exchange of data within the statistical system for statistical purposes.

This new approach to confidentiality protection and exchange is critical to the efficient operation and coordination of the federal statistical system. *No other single action could do as much to reduce the cost of unnecessary data collection and to improve the data series produced.* In order to ensure that such exchange actually takes place, however, it is important that the legislation provide clear authorization for data exchange upon request of a user agency, and that the confidentiality of the data exchanged be ensured. "Firewall" provisions are critically important; the law will need to be written carefully so as to make certain that the data cannot be used for regulation or enforcement activity. Provision will also need to be made for development of written agreements—to be signed by each of the agency heads participating in data exchange, and for review by OMB's Chief Statistician—to protect data confidentiality and to provide guidelines for settling any disputes that might arise between agencies in the system over the exchange arrangements.

Special provisions will also be required to meet the needs of federal-state cooperative programs. Considerable thought has already been given to this issue and wording has been drafted by the Bureau of Labor Statistics, which has the most extensive cooperative arrangements with individual states for the collection of data. Only limited information will be required to be shared with the states, but regulations will need to be written to ensure that data in the hands of the states are adequately protected from identifiable release.

All survey data collected by agencies in the system would be covered by the law. But it is important for the legislation to go further than that. It should also include provisions for the exchange of both household and business lists, with special arrangements designed specifically to deal with them.

The quality of the government's database could be enormously enhanced, probably at reduced cost as well, if a single agency were made responsible for industry coding, a single agency for occupational coding, etc., and the results used as a single microcoded system by each of the statistical agencies. It would be possible, for example, to reduce the cost of classification system revisions, to develop a single universe or list of business establishments to be used across the system for survey sample selection, to advance research on local area data improvement, and even to ferret out duplication of effort that has so far been undetectable.

A complicating factor in the exchange of business list information is the fact that the Bureau of the Census receives information from the tax records from the Internal Revenue Service. Arrangements to permit the exchange of such data require further consideration, but the issue should not be allowed to prevent data sharing now. This may only be a question of timing. The National Statistical Improvement Act, a law covering the entire statistical system, should be passed first. Because of the complex system of laws governing the various statistical agencies, however, it will be necessary to amend several of the existing laws governing the practice of particular agencies within the system. Once this has been accomplished, the Chief Statistician, with the help of a working group representing the agencies involved, can propose specific legislation to address the unique IRS legislative issue. Meanwhile, the Bureau of the Census should keep the IRS data separate from other data on the business list, so that those data can be exchanged with other agencies when the need arises.

Standardization of Agency Status Within Departments

Federal statistical agencies come in many shapes and sizes. Comparison reveals more differences than similarities, and many of these differences affect the efficiency of the agency's operation. Some agency heads are appointed by the President with consent of the Senate, and some are career civil servants. Some presidentially-appointed agency heads have fixed terms of office, and some do not. Several have independent agency status within their own department, and some do not. As a result, operational effectiveness is affected by differences in public perception, executive branch status, and the ability to deal with Congress. The proposed National Statistical Improvement Act must deal with these issues if we are to improve the operation and efficiency of the federal statistical system.

Standardization of Appointments

Perhaps the two most important attributes of statistical agency leadership are longevity and independence from political pressure. The five agency heads that are career civil servants tend to have longevity; they remain in office for long periods of time, covering more than one Presidential term of office. These agencies also have some general protection from political pressure (since they remain civil servants). Their ability to resist demands for changes in the way the data are interpreted is limited by the fact that they can easily be transferred to another position in the parent department. In general, however, the career status arrangement has worked well, for example at BEA and at NASS, and probably does not need to be changed.

The same cannot be said for the presidentially-appointed agency heads. Of the five agencies whose heads are appointed by the President with the consent of the Senate, only three—BLS, NCES, and BTS— have fixed terms of office; these heads by law serve a four-year term. By contrast, the directors of the Bureaus of the Census and Justice Statistics and of the Energy Information Administration serve at the pleasure of the President and routinely resign when a new President takes office so that a new political appointment can be made. These agency heads should have the same legislative protection against political influence as those at BLS, NCES, and BTS. The proposed statistical legislation should provide that presidentially-appointed statistical agency heads have a fixed term of office. The law could adopt the BLS practice of a 4-year term, although a 5-year term might be more practical given the planning and operational cycle for the population census. In any case, the appointment should not coincide exactly with the term of the President.

The tenure of a statistical agency head is important for other reasons as well. In addition to protection from political interference, the length of time in office has an important effect on the efficiency with which a statistical agency operates. Statistical programs require long lead time from planning to execution, and it takes some time for even the best of agency heads to grasp fully the intricacies of the many survey programs undertaken by the federal system. I served as Commissioner of Labor Statistics for three full four-year terms. During that period, the Bureau of the Census had seven leadership changes—four directors plus three periods between directors when a deputy served as acting director for periods of some length.

Standardization of Statistical Agency Status Within Cabinet Departments

The proposed legislation should also standardize and upgrade the reporting relationship of the directors of statistical agencies within each department and provide for their full control of resources allocated to them by Congress. Both the status of an agency in a department and the reporting level of its director are critical to the importance of an agency and the strength with which it can operate in the government bureaucracy. It is important for the director of a statistical agency to be fully involved in the development of the budget for the agency, and to have the resources for the agency listed as a line item in the Congressional budget. This is not now consistently done across the statistical system.

The new law should also establish a rule that statistical agency heads hold rank at the Assistant Secretary level (as is the case at the Department of Labor) and have direct access to the head of that agency. At the present time, some of the statistical agencies control their own resources and defend them before Congress, but some do not. Statistical agencies should act as the statistical arms of their departments. They cannot carry out this function effectively without an elevation in their status.

Codification of Procedures for the Release of Major Economic Indicators and Extension of the Procedures to Social Indicators

Quick access to government data is becoming increasingly important as the knowledge gained from analysis of data becomes more useful. Because of the potential political uses of data, however, it is essential that all data users be assured equal access in a timely way. The current system for the release of such sensitive data series as the national accounts, employment and unemployment data, inflation indexes and other major economic series works quite well. But the release system should have a legislative foundation. A system used to ensure the objectivity and equal access to data produced by the government should not be based on an executive order that can be changed without action of the Congress. The National Statistical Improvement Act should codify the existing system for the release of major economic indicators and extend the same system to the release of major social indicators, most notably statistics on poverty, on the state of the nation's education, and on its health.

Strengthening the Role of OMB's Chief Statistician

The new statistical law should make clear that the chief statistician at OMB serves as the head of the U.S. statistical system and has the authority to coordinate statistical work in the government, to ensure its quality and objectivity, and to represent it abroad. The chief statistician should be appointed by the President with the consent of the Senate and have a fixed term of office. In addition, the law should provide for the chief statistician to have a direct reporting relationship to the Director of OMB. These changes are required to provide the chief statistician with the status and the authority necessary to carry out the responsibilities effectively.

But more than that needs to be done. The National Statistical Improvement Act should also recognize the need for the resources required for the chief statistician to carry out the assigned responsibilities, either by creating a Federally Funded Research and Development Center (FFRDC) to assist the chief statistician and the small statistical policy staff, or by funding and establishing a special research center for this work through the National Science Foundation (NSF). Unless there is a Central Statistical Board, the statistical policy group must be located in OMB, so that it can provide leadership to the statistical system and have authority to establish priorities among the conflicting demands of a decentralized statistical system. That is a big job which can only be done well with sufficient resources to do the oversight and research required. In my view, however, it is neither practical nor desirable to increase the statistical policy group staff to carry out all of these functions. It would be far more efficient to provide each year, through the budget process, a small group of professionals (perhaps 20 permanent employees) to handle day-to-day operations and to provide the chief statistician with the ability to call upon an FFRDC or a specialized Research Center to undertake specific projects that require specialized personnel. A Federally Funded Research and Development Center is a research group which performs research only for the government agency for which it was created and must meet certain legislative requirements to ensure that the work could not normally be done by the staff of the agency itself. Most of the FFRDCs do defense research, but a few work in other areas. In recent years, NSF has created Research Centers in several scientific areas which specialize in a particular area of scientific research. NSF has funded these Centers, which, in most cases, are located at universities.

The new statistical legislation should provide for the initial capitalization of the FFRDC or Research Center by authorizing the annual appropriation of $2.0 to $4.0 million for this purpose in the budget of the NSF. As in the case of the Joint Statistical Center for the training of statistical agency personnel now located at the University of Maryland, the funding and selection of the statistical FFRDC or creation of a new Research Center can best be implemented through the National Science Foundation. NSF would be responsible for the scientific selection process in consultation with the chief statistician who would provide the necessary information for preparation of the request for bids.

Creation of this research capability to provide expert advice and technical resources required to accomplish the research needed for statistical policy formulation makes great sense. The statistical policy need clearly fits the requirements for this type of funding. The activities to be performed include analyzing, integrating, and performing supporting and applied research. The normal contracting process cannot produce the kind of team needed for objective and timely research involving the integration of data, establishment of a unified database with data integrated across the system which could service all users, as well as specific projects in application of new statistical and survey techniques, use of new technological capacity and economies of scale. Since the chief statistician has system-wide responsibilities for managing, monitoring, and overseeing statistics on a government-wide basis, legislative requirements for establishment of an FFRDC are met. Alternatively, the research requirements of the statistical system are sufficiently innovative and unique that they are consistent with NSF experience in the creation of specialized Research Centers. The tasks which need to be performed require specially qualified personnel. They cannot be performed by private sector companies, both because of potential conflict of interest problems and because of the need to use confidential data in carrying out successful research. The new law should provide for an Advisory Council to assist the chief statistician in overseeing the FFRDC or make provision for scientific advice in the case of an NSF Research Center. Provision should also be made for funding special projects by other agencies in the system, when deemed advisable by the chief statistician. (See table 7.1)

It is quite clear that the important statistical policy role I envision cannot be carried out by a small staff at OMB. Indeed, the kind of work that needs to be done to integrate survey programs and data, to

Table 7.1 ELEMENTS OF THE NATIONAL STATISTICAL IMPROVEMENT ACT

A. UNIFORM PROTECTION OF CONFIDENTIALITY

Replace individual agency confidentiality laws and orders with a single, uniform system that guarantees confidentiality across the agencies of government with the production of statistics as their major mission

Permit the sharing of confidential data for *statistical purposes* within the protected system

Explicit prohibition against the use of data collected under pledge of confidentiality by statistical agencies to be used in regulation and enforcement

Special arrangements permitting sharing of confidential data for statistical purposes (necessary for the operation of the cooperative program) with state agencies cooperating with federal agencies in statistical programs

Questions involving interpretation of the legal provisions of the law are to be decided by the Chief Statistician of OMB

Protection of the law and the exchange of data under it includes universe lists as well as survey micro-data

Requirement that the Chief Statistician of OMB monitor procedures and oversee procedures used to protect confidentiality by the agencies within the system; Chief Statistician also to have the authority to create a Confidentiality Advisory Committee if deemed desirable

B. CODIFICATION OF RELEASE PROCEDURES FOR MAJOR ECONOMIC AND SOCIAL INDICATORS

Codify the arrangements of the OMB order on the release of major economic indicators so that the requirements are based on law rather than on executive order

Extend legal protection to the procedures for the release of major social indicators, including such releases as those on poverty and on the state of the nation's education and health

Provide authority for OMB's Chief Statistician to include new indicators in the protected release procedures as they develop

C. PROVIDE GREATER UNIFORMITY OF STATISTICAL AGENCY STATUS

Provide that the head of the statistical agency within a department of government have direct access to the head of the department, either through a direct reporting status or through a legislated right of access

Require that each part of the federal statistical system legally be a separate agency within its department with authority over the budget appropriated for the agency by the Congress and for control of full-time permanent personnel slots approved by the Congress and the Administration through the budget process

Heads of large statistical agencies to be appointed by the President with the consent of the Senate for a fixed term of office (preferably 5 years) or to be career members of the Senior Executive Service

(continued)

Table 7.1 ELEMENTS OF THE NATIONAL STATISTICAL IMPROVEMENT ACT
(continued)

D. STRENGTHEN OMB'S CHIEF STATISTICIAN

Statistical forms clearance at OMB are to be separated from regulatory forms clearance. All statistical forms are to be cleared by the Chief Statistician of OMB

Chief Statistician of OMB is to be appointed by the President with the consent of the Senate and should serve a fixed term of office, similar to the arrangements for the Comptroller General of the United States

Provide for the creation of a Federally Funded Research and Development Center (FFRDC) or other scientific research group for statistics. Authorize appropriation of $2.0 to $4.0 million annually for the statistical FFRDC in the budget of the National Science Foundation which would assist in evaluation of bids for the establishment of the Center. The Chief Statistician of OMB would have oversight responsibility for the Center whose major role would be to assist the Chief Statistician and other parts of the federal statistical system as determined by the Chief Statistician.

develop new approaches to survey design to improve the quality and the relevance of government data, and to assist the chief statistician in solving the problems of our widely decentralized system requires far more expertise than can be expected to reside in the statistical policy group. The use of a statistical FFRDC or Research Center with the capacity to do specialized research could go far toward eliminating many of the problems caused by the increasing fragmentation of the U.S. statistical system. It would also help enhance the quality of the U.S. statistical system and increase its competitiveness with the systems in other countries. These are now investing more than ever before in the development of useful data for policy formulation and evaluation.

* * *

All the improvements I have discussed are important. But none will be very effective unless this country decides to enhance and support the statistical policy and coordination function which stands at the hub of its statistical system. The best way to do this is to move it organizationally into a unit which can provide the necessary stature and resources to assist the federal statistical system to carry out its responsibilities. If such an organizational change should not prove to be a practical option, then strong legislative action is required to enhance its prestige, authority, and resources.

Through their recent votes, the American people have indicated a desire, indeed an appetite, for change in government structure and operation. Since accurate and objective data of high quality are essential to the operation of any democratic system, part of that change should take place in the organizational structure of the federal agencies which produce the statistical information which inform our citizens and their government.

Note

1. At the very least, such legislation would need to be considered by the Committees in the House and in the Senate which are concerned with a) the Department of Labor, b) the Department of Commerce, and c) the Committees dealing with government operations in general as well as by d) the appropriations subcommittees dealing with the Departments containing statistical agencies.

REFERENCES

A Framework for Planning U.S. Federal Statistics for the 1980s. U.S. Department of Commerce, Office of Federal Statistical Policy and Standards. Washington, D.C. 1978.

Anderson, Margo J., *The American Census. A Social History.* Yale University Press. 1988.

————, "The 1990 Census: How Good Is It?", *Government Publications Review*, vol. 19. 1992.

Alonso, William and Paul Starr, eds., *The Politics of Numbers*, Russell Sage Foundation, New York, 1987.

Atkinson, Richard C. and and Gregg B. Jackson, ed., *Research and Education Reform, Roles for the Office of Educational Research and Improvement.* Committee on the Federal Role in Education. National Academy Press. May 1992.

Barabba, Vincent P, Richard O. Mason and Ian I. Mitroff, "Federal Statistics in a Complex: The Case of the 1980 Census," *American Statistician*, vol. 37 no. 3, August 1983.

Baseline Data Corporation, *The Federal Statistical System 1980–1985*, A Report prepared for the Congressional Research Service of the Library of Congress, Committee on Government Operations, 98th Congress, 2d session, 1984.

Bell, Ruth, "The Establishment of the Office of Federal Statistical Policy and Standards," *Statistical Reporter*, no. 78-1, October 1977.

Bonnen, James T., "Federal Statistical Coordination Today: A Disaster or a Disgrace?", Milbank Memorial Fund Quarterly, *Health and Society*, vol. 62, no. 1. 1984.

————, "A Record of the 1978–80 White House 'Federal Statistical Reorganization Project", Department of Agricultural Economics, Michigan State University, Staff Paper no. 94-75, November 1994.

Bradburn, Norman M., "The Relationship of Federal to Private Statistics," Paper at meetings of Evaluation Research Society, Baltimore, Md., October 29, 1982.

Business Week, June 3, 1991, November 7, 1994.

Castles, Ian, "Responding to User Needs", *Journal of the Royal Statistical Society* (Series A), vol. 154, part 1. 1991.

Cecil, Joe S., "Confidentiality Legislation and the United States Federal Statistical System", *Journal of Official Statistics*, vol. 9, no. 2, 1993.

Clague, Ewan, *The Bureau of Labor Statistics*. New York, Praeger. 1968.

Coffey, Jerry and Hermann Habermann, "Federal-State-Local Relationships: Where Are We? Where Are We Going?". Joint Statistical Meetings, Annaheim, California. 1990.

Congressional Research Service, *Federal Statistics and National Needs*. Subcommittee on Energy, Nuclear Proliferation and Government Processes of the Committee on Governmental Affairs. U.S. Senate. 1983.

"Coordination in Federal Statistics Gathering Programs, a Staff Study," Committee on Post Office and Civil Service, House of Representatives, 95th Congress, 1st session, January 27, 1977.

Creating a Center for Education Statistics: A Time for Action. Committee on National Statistics Panel to Evaluate the National Center for Education Statistics. Washington, D.C. National Academy Press. 1986.

de Muth, Christopher, "Federal Statistical Coordination Today, Comments," *American Statistician*, vol. 37, no. 3, August 1983.

Duncan, George T., Thomas B. Jabine, and Virginia A. de Wolf, ed., *Private Lives and Public Policies*. Panel on Confidentiality and Data Access, Committee on National Statistics. National Academy Press, Washington, D.C. 1993.

Duncan, Joseph W., "Planning for Statistical Developments in the Twenty-First Century", *Business Economics*, October 1992.

———and Theodore Clemence, "Arguments For and Against a Decentralized Federal Statistical System", *Statistical Reporter*, no. 82-3. December 1981.

———and Andrew C. Gross, *Statistics for the 21st Century*. New York, Dun & Bradstreet Corporation. 1993.

———and William C. Shelton, *Revolution in United States Government Statistics 1926–1976*. U.S. Department of Commerce, Office of Federal Statistical Policy and Standards. 1978.

———, "The Federal Statististical System in Historical Perspective", Los Angeles, California, August 14, 1975.

Eckler, A. Ross, *The Bureau of the Census*. New York, Praeger, 1972.

Economist. 1990–1994.

Federal Statistics, Report of the President' s Commission, volumes I and II, Washington, 1971.

Felligi, Ivan P. "Maintaining Public Confidence in Official Statistics", *Journal of the Royal Statististical Society* (Series A), vol. 154, part 1. 1991.

Fienberg, Stephen E., "Innovative Statistical Methodology Enables 'Counting with Confidence' ", *Journal of the Royal Statistical Society* (Series A), vol. 154, part 1. 1991.

———, "Federal Statistical Coordination Today, Comments," *The American Statistician*, vol. 37, no. 3, August 1983..

————, "Conflicts Between the Needs for Access to Statistical Information and Demands for Confidentiality," *Journal of Official Statistics*, vol. 10, no. 2. 1994.

Formaini, Robert, *The Myth of Scientific Public Policy*, Transaction Publishers, New Brunswick, N.J., 1990.

Fuller, Wayne, "Masking Procedures for Microdata Disclosure Limitation", *Journal of Official Statistics*, vol. 9, no. 2, 1993.

————, "Conflicts Between the Needs for Access to Statistical Information and Demands for Confidentiality," *Journal of Official Statistics*, vol. 10, no. 2, 1994.

Franchet, Yves, "International Comparability of Statistics: Background, Harmonization Principles and Present Issues", *Journal of the Royal Statistical Society* (Series A), vol. 154, part 1. 1991.

Gillette, Clayton P. and Thomas D. Hopkins, "Federal User Fees: A Legal and Economic Analysis," *Boston University Law Review*. November 1987.

Government Statistical Services. Command 8236. London, Her Majesty's Stationery Office. April 1981. (Raynor Report.)

Government Statistics, a Report of the Committee on Government Statistics and Information Services, Social Science Research Council, Bulletin 26. New York. April 1937.

Grossman, Jonathon, *The Department of Labor*. New York, Praeger. 1973.

Hauser, Robert M., "Educational and Social Mobility: Data Needs for the Twenty-First Century," Remarks prepared for a forum, Socioeconomic Data Needs for the Twenty-First Century, 1993 meetings of the American Association for the Advancement of Science, Boston, February 11, 1993.

Hibbert, J., "Public Confidence in the Integrity and Validity of Official Statistics", *Journal of the Royal Statistical Society* (Series A), vol. 153, part 2. 1990.

Improving the Federal Statistical System: Issues and Options. President's Reorganization Project for the Federal Statistical System. Washington, D.C., February 1981.

Innes, Judith Eleanor, *Knowledge and Public Policy: The Search for Meaningful Indicators*. Rutgers University. 1990.

Jabine, Thomas B., "Statistical Disclosure Limitation Practices of United States Statistical Agencies", *Journal of Official Statistics*, vol. 9, no. 2, 1993.

————, "Procedures for Restricted Data Access", *Journal of Official Statistics*, vol. 9, no. 2, 1993.

Johansson, Sten, "Information Needs for the Market and for Democracy," *Journal of Official Statistics*, vol. 6, no. 1, 1990.

Jones, Sidney L., "Economic Perceptions and Realities", Shirley Kallek Memorial Lecture, Research Conference of the Bureau of the Census. Washington, D.C. 1993.

Juster, Thomas F., "The State of U.S. Economic Statistics: Current and Prospective Quality, Policy Needs, and Resources". American Economic Association Committee on the Quality of Economic Statistics. Conference of Research on Income and Wealth. Washington, D.C. May 1988.

Lambert, Diane, "Measures of Disclosure Risk and Harm", *Journal of Official Statistics,* vol. 9, no. 2, 1993.

Leiby, James, *Carroll Wright and Labor Reform: The Origin of Labor Statistics.* Harvard University. 1960.

Little, Roderick J.A., "Statistical Analysis of Masked Data", *Journal of Official Statistics,* vol. 9, no. 2, 1993.

Martin, George, *Madam Secretary, Frances Perkins.* 1976.

Martin, Margaret E., "Statistical Practice in Bureaucracies", *Journal of the American Statistical Association,* vol. 76, no. 373. 1981.

_____and Miron L. Straf, ed., *Principles and Practices for a Federal Statistical Agency.* Washington, D.C., National Academy Press. 1992.

Meeks, Ronald L., "A Review of Some of the Major Statistical Agencies Within the U.S. Federal Statistical System", *Statistical Reporter,* no. 80–9, June 1980.

Mills, F. C. and Clarence Long, *The Statistical Agencies of the United States Government.* New York, National Bureau of Economic Research. 1940.

Morrison, Sylvia, *Federal Economic Statistics: Would Closer Coordination Make for Better Numbers?,* Congressional Research Service Report for Congress, Washington, D.C., November 4, 1992.

Moser, Claus, "The Role of the Central Statistical Office in Assisting Public Policy Makers", *American Statistician,* vol. 30, no. 2. May 1976.

Mugge, Robert H., "Informed Consent in U.S. Government Surveys", *Journal of Official Statistics,* vol. 9, no. 2, 1993.

Norwood, Janet L., "Should those who Produce Statistics Analyze them? How Far Should Analysis Go? An American View", *Bulletin of the International Statistical Institute,* vol. 46, Proceedings 40th session. 1975.

_____, "The Influence of Statistics on Public Policy", Proceedings of the Symposium on Statistics in Science, Industry and Public Policy. Washington, D.C., National Academy Press. 1989.

_____, "Statistics and Public Policy: Reflections of a Changing World", *Journal of the American Statistical Association,* vol. 85, no. 409, 1980.

_____, "Data Policy and Politics in a Democracy", *Journal of Economic Education,* vol. 25, no. 3. 1994.

_____, "Measuring Unemployment: A Change in the Yardstick", *Policy Bites,* The Urban Institute, no. 21, March 1994.

_____and Judith M. Tanur, "Measuring Unemployment in the Nineties", *Public Opinion Quarterly,* vol. 58, 1994.

"Official Statistics: Counting with Confidence", Working Party on Official Statistics in the United Kingdom, *Journal of the Royal Statistical Society* (Series A), vol. 154, part 1, 1991.

OMB 1994. See *Statistical Programs of the United States*.

Paperwork Reduction. Washington, D.C. General Accounting Office. December 1993.

Pearson, Robert W., "Social Statistics and an American Urban Underclass: Improving the Knowledge Base for Social Policy in the 1990's", *Journal of the American Statistical Association*, June 1991.

Raynor Report. See Government Statistical Services 1981.

"Report of the Joint Ad Hoc Committee on Government Statistics", *Statistical Reporter*, September 1976.

Report of the Committee on Environment and Public Works, "The Surface Transportation Efficiency Act of 1991, U.S. Senate, 102d Congress, 1st session, Report 102–71. Washington. 1991.

"Report of Statistical Society Meeting on Public Confidence in the Integrity and Validity of Official Statistics", *Journal of the Royal Statistical Society* (Series A), vol. 153, part 2, 1990.

Report of the Statistics Committee of the National Association of Business Economists. February 1988.

Reynolds, Paul D., "Privacy and Advances in Social and Policy Sciences: Balancing Present Costs and Future Gains", *Journal of Official Statistics*, vol. 9, no. 2, 1993.

Ryten, Jacob, "Statistical Organization Criteria for Inter-Country Comparisons and their Application to Canada", *Journal of Official Statistics*, vol. 6, no. 3, 1990.

Setting Statistical Priorities. Committee on National Statistics Panel on Methodology for Statistical Priorities. NTIS (PB 256–434). 1976.

Singer, Eleanor, "Informed Consent and Survey Response: A Summary of the Empirical Literature", *Journal of Official Statistics*, vol. 9, no. 2, 1993.

75 Years and Counting, A History of Statistics Canada. Ottawa, Statistics Canada. 1993.

Slater, Courtenay, "Federal Statistical Coordination Today, Comment," *American Statistician*, vol.37 no. 3, August 1983.

Statistical Needs for a Changing Economy—Background Paper. Washington, D.C. Office of Technology Assessment. September 1989.

Statistical Programs of the United States. Executive Office of the President, Office of Management and Budget (OMB). Issues for Fiscal Years 1980–94.

Statistical Reorganization. Committee on Statistical Reorganization. Washington, D.C. 1908.

Status of the Statistical Community After Sustaining Budget Reductions, General Accounting Office, Washington, D.C. July 1984.

Straf, Miron, "A Conversation with Margaret Martin", *Statistical Science*, vol. 9, no. 1, 1994.

Surface Transportation Efficiency Act of 1991, Report of the Committee on Environment and Public Works, U.S. Senate, 102nd Congress, 1st session, Report 102-71, Washington, 1991.

Sy, Karen J. and Alice Robbin, "Federal Statistical Policies and Programs: How Good are the Numbers?", *Annual Review of Information Science and Technology*, vol 25, 1990.

The Organization of National Statistical Services: A Review of Major Issues. United Nations, Studies in Methods, Series F, No. 21. New York. 1977.

The Coordination and Integration of Government Statistical Programs, Report of the Subcommittee on Economic Statistics of the Joint Economic Committee, 90th Congress 1st session, Washington, D.C., 1967.

Triplett, Jack, "The Federal Statistical System's Response to Emerging Data Needs", *Journal of Economic and Social Measurement*, vol. 17, 1991.

Wallman, Katherine K., "The Statistical System Under Stress", August 12, 1988.

_____, "Federal Statistical Coordination Today. An Epilogue as Prologue", *American Statistician*, vol. 37, no. 3, August 1983.

_____, "Politics and Statistics: Reassessing the Mix", 1983.

ABOUT THE AUTHOR

Janet L. Norwood is a Senior Fellow at the Urban Institute. She also serves as Chair of the Advisory Council on Unemployment Compensation, to which she was appointed by President Bush and reappointed by President Clinton. From 1979–1991, she was the U.S. Commissioner of the Bureau of Labor Statistics (BLS). She has written extensively on statistical issues and has testified often before Congress' Joint Economic Committee and before the committees on Labor and Human Resources, Finance, and Government Operations. She is an elected honorary Fellow of the Royal Statistical Society, American Association for the Advancement of Science, National Association of Business Economists, and the American Statistical Association, of which she is Past President.